Feb. 1992

To Mum and Dad with love
and best wishes from Gavin.

THE HISTORICAL AND CULTURAL CONNECTIONS AND PARALLELS BETWEEN WALES AND AUSTRALIA

Edited by

Gavin Edwards and Graham Sumner

Welsh Studies
Volume 4

The Edwin Mellen Press
Lewiston/Queenston/Lampeter

Library of Congress Cataloging-in-Publication Data

The Historical and cultural connections and parallels between Wales
and Australia / edited by Gavin Edwards and Graham Sumner.
     p.   cm. -- (Welsh studies ; v. 4)
   Enlarged and edited versions of papers presented at Wales and
Australia: a Symposium, organized by the Centre for Australian
Studies in Wales, St. David's University College, Lampeter, Wales,
1988.
   Includes bibliographical references.
   ISBN 0-7734-9716-1
   1. Australia--Relations--Wales--Congresses. 2. Wales--Relations-
-Australia--Congresses. 3. Welsh--Australia--History--Congresses.
I. Edwards, Gavin. II. Sumner, Graham N. III. Wales and Australia:
a Symposium (1988 : Centre for Australian Studies in Wales, St.
David's University College) IV. St. David's University College
(Lampeter, Wales). Centre for Australian Studies in Wales.
V. Series.
DU113.5.G7H57 1991
303.48'2940429--dc20   91-18986
                                               CIP

This is volume 4 in the continuing series
Welsh Studies
Volume 4 ISBN 0-7734-9716-1
WS Series ISBN 0-88946-479-0

A CIP catalog record for this book
is available from the British Library.

The Edwin Mellen Press   The Edwin Mellen Press
Box 450   Box 67
Lewiston, New York   Queenston, Ontario
USA 14092   CANADA L0S 1L0

The Edwin Mellen Press, Ltd.
Lampeter, Dyfed, Wales
UNITED KINGDOM SA48 7DY

Printed in the United States of America

THE HISTORICAL AND CULTURAL CONNECTIONS AND PARALLELS BETWEEN WALES AND AUSTRALIA

CONTENTS

THE GENESIS OF AUSTRALIAN STUDIES

Don Grant

[Associate Professor Don Grant teaches in the School of Communication and Cultural Studies at Curtin University, Perth, Western Australia. In 1974 he established the first Australian Studies major in any degree course in Australia. He was foundation Director of Curtin's Centre for Australian Studies, co-founder of the Australian Studies Association, and has been co-editor of <u>Australian Studies</u> (formerly <u>Australian Studies Bulletin</u>) since its birth in 1984.]

There is something grand, profound, Biblical, about the title 'The Genesis of Australian Studies'. At the genesis of the title itself, Carl Bridge, who was lurking in the background in the Australian Studies Centre at the University of London, immediately suggested an alternative title - 'The Exodus of Australian Studies'. Carl was joking, of course, but his implied point must be taken seriously.

How solid is the present interest in Australian Studies? How deep is the commitment of those academics and teachers in Australia who wish to 'Australianise the curriculum' in the ways recommended in the report of the Committee to review Australian Studies in Tertiary Education

(CRASTE)? [1]   How strong are the reactionary forces in the universities, the worshippers of the traditional disciplines, many of them at the most senior levels in the tertiary education system, who sneer scornfully or nod paternally at the very notion of Australian Studies?   How committed are those Australianists abroad to their task? How much support do they get within their own universities?   How much encouragement are they likely to receive in the future from government and organisations in Australia?   Is it possible that the present forward surge of Australian studies will be arrested when the brouhaha of the 1988 Bicentennial celebrations dies away?   These questions are, of course, as relevant to the Centre for Australian Studies in Wales - the host for the Symposium which eventually led to the production of this book - as they are for all Australian Studies Centres and Australianists around the world.

Always an optimist, I rejected the Exodus title. Although my present theme is 'Genesis', I trust that in a few years' time a more appropriate theme might be 'The Revelations of Australian Studies'.

So began a paper I delivered at the University of Wales Geography Colloquium held at Lampeter on 18 May 1988.

I have frequently been asked, both at home in Australia and while overseas, what is Australian Studies?   There is no one answer. Australian Studies has a different meaning for teachers in Australia from the meaning it has for teachers in English speaking countries abroad, and different again from its meaning in non-English speaking countries. But within these three divisions there are also many meanings and a variety of perspectives. Writing from an Australian perspective, I feel much the same as did Humphrey McQueen, a member of CRASTE, when he attempted to compile a list of items which might be included in a common core curriculum for Australian Studies. Humphrey wrote:

> I have only the haziest notion of either a geological or a mythological account of the origins of Uluru. Nor could I begin to frame ideas to go into a common core of knowledge from Australia's botanical or geological realms.
>
> Never have I been more aware of the boundlessness of my ignorance than on the September afternoon in 1985 when I climbed Obiri Rock to see creation spread out before me. On the way up I had passed Aboriginal rock art whose significance I accepted without being able to explain. From the peak, I could see the Arnhem Land escarpment, the flood plain, a row of rock outlyers and the serpentine rivers. All about me were birds, plants and marine life of whose ecology I knew next to nothing." (2)

I also have been to Obiri Rock; have stood on the edge of the Great Sandy Desert in the Pilbara region of Western Australia; have travelled by boat in Kakadu National Park and along the Daintree River; have stood in snow on the Central Highlands of Tasmania, have explored the Sydney Opera House, the National War Memorial in

Canberra and the convict prison at Port Arthur.   I've also read
Colleen McCullough's The Thorn Birds and Patrick White's Voss and
watched Paul Hogan's film Crocodile Dundee.   My ignorances
about Australia are as boundless as are Humphrey McQueen's.
Which is why I agree with Humphrey when he writes of the necessity
for an Australian curriculum which will challenge 'certain entrenched
perceptions of excellence in education, and effectiveness in economic
life.'

> An Australian curriculum [he goes on] is part of the
> creativity that we will need if we are not to be
> categorised along with the sparrow, the starling and
> the prickly pear as destructive interlopers. By
> seeking to ensure that Australians will never again be
> foreigners in our own culture, an Australian
> curriculum challenges us to accept that this continent
> is where we must work if we are to make it home.

Humphrey might also have mentioned that other interloper, the rabbit,
which has adapted so readily to Australian conditions.   Why is it, I've
been asking myself, while driving through the green and pleasant lands
of England, Scotland and Wales, that the rabbit has not mutiplied here
to the plague proportions that it did in Australia?   I suppose the
answer has something to do with nature's balance.   The continent of
Australia had few defences against the interlopers from Europe,
whether winged, spiky, four-footed, or two-footed.   For nearly 200
years the country absorbed them and, in the case of the two-footed

variety, made the values, the history, the education curricula of the emigrant countries the bases of civilisation in the newly settled country.

The Australian Studies movement (to give an inflated title to what still remains a small, but increasing, number of individual initiatives) in Australia, is, I believe, one of the most significant developments yet to have occurred in the Australian education system, with effects yet to be determined on the Australian consciousness.

The recent interest in Australian Studies has not resulted from, nor in, heightened xenophobia, jingoism or ocker nationalism - although these traits exist in Australia as they do in all countries. It arises from something much more deeply-rooted, something perhaps which has taken 200 years to break through the surface of that ancient land. At the same time that international political, economic and power shifts have forced Australia to look inwards to itself rather than outwards to others for solutions and decisions, the Australian people themselves have begun to re-write their history in their own terms and to ponder seriously their future role in the world as Australians.

Coincidental with these internal Australian contemplations has been an increasing interest in Australian Studies in dozens of countries in Europe, North America and Asia. Centres for Austarlian Studies have been established at universities as far apart as Shanghai and Pennsylvania, and as close as London and Lampeter. Courses in

Australian Studies are now taught at about 100 universities outside Australia. Academics and post-graduate students come to Australia in increasing numbers to study, attend conferences, and as Visiting Fellows. The reverse is also true. The growth abroad of interest in Australian Studies has also provided an opportunity for Australian scholars to contribute to and learn from the programmes in overseas centres. Thus the Australian Studies movement has worked to foster two-way exchanges and, one would hope, to increase knowledge and understanding between countries.

'Wales and Australia: A Symposium', the first symposium organised by the Centre for Australian Studies in Wales at St. David's University College, Lampeter, was indicative of what is occurring. Four of the papers were presented by people based in Wales, two by Australians. All papers, ranging through migration, historiography, broadcasting and mining, sought to establish historical and cultural connections between Wales and Australia. The symposium itself was generally agreed to be very informative and successful. The papers presented have been enlarged and edited for publication in this form.

The establishment of the Centre for Australian Studies in Wales and its location at a small university college in a remote (if anywhere in Wales can be called remote by Australian standards), little town is itself a matter deserving comment. Inaugurated in 1986, the Centre's aims are to initiate and coordinate research in Australia and the Australia-Wales connection, to coordinate and organise events, lectures, seminars, etc., in Wales, and to establish exchanges between institutions in the two countries. The director of the Centre, Dr. Graham Sumner, is a geographer; other members of the management committee come from the areas of English, History, Philosophy and Welsh studies. Already, through the Wales and Australia symposium and subsequent gatherings, through visits both ways between the staff in the Centre and Australian academics, and through various publications, the Centre for Australian Studies in Wales has established itself as one of the most lively and optimistic focuses for Australian Studies abroad.

I wish I could say the same about the future of Australian Studies in other parts of Britain. The Sir Robert Gordon Menzies Centre for Australian Studies at the University of London (no longer funded by the Australian Government, but by the Menzies Foundation) remains the pivot for Australian Studies in the United Kingdom, and the British Australian Studies Association (BASA) retains a nucleus of enthusiasts. But when I attended the BASA conference at Lincoln in June 1988, there seemed to be a feeling of dejection emanating from some Australianists who had worked so hard to get their courses going. Perhaps this was simply part of the general sense of helplessness felt by people in the British universities, particularly those in the Humanities and Social Sciences, as draconian government policies cut away. Without wishing in any way to countenance such policies by the British Government, I should point out that the same general policies are at work also in Australia, North America, and other European countries I visited.   It's just that the sword seems to be biting deeper in Britain than elsewhere, and areas on the fringe, as Australian Studies remains, are easy targets for the scissors.

I wish, too, that I could hold out hope for greater responsiveness by the Australian Government for the support of Australian Studies abroad. The Department of Foreign Affairs and Trade have focused their main attention on Asia (perhaps they are correct), while still supporting Australian Studies initiatives (to a lesser extent) in other parts of the world.   In my view the Department remains short-sighted in the low priority it gives to fostering cultural connections in overseas countries (cultural attachés are not common in Australian Embassies).   I was disappointed also that in *Windows Onto Worlds*, the report of the Committee to Review Australian Studies in Tertiary Education, so little emphasis was placed on the desirability of encouraging Australian Studies initiatives in overseas countries.

It is not fitting to end on a gloomy note. Both in academe and in government, situations remain volatile. Positive action can induce positive responses.   This book, coming from a most unlikely source, is an example of positive action.   It will be welcomed by Australian Studies practitioners, and might, if it can be distributed widely, reach some of those people who will have direct influence on the future of Australian Studies, in Australia and abroad, during the next few years.

Notes

1. <u>Windows onto Worlds</u>. Report of the Committee to Review Australian Studies in Tertiary Education, Canberra, 1987.

2. Humphrey McQueen, <u>Teaching an Australian Curriculum,</u> 1987 paper.

GWLAD YR AUR;

NEU,

GYDYMAITH YR YMFUDWR CYMREIG

I.

AUSTRALIA:

YN CYNWYS

Hanes y Cyfandir Australaidd, y Trefedigaethau Prydeinig ynddo, ac Ardaloedd yr Aur, eu Tir, Hinsawdd, Masnach, Cyflogau, Deddfau, &c., &c.; yn nghyda lluaws o Ffeithiau o ddyddordeb a phwys arbenig i'r Ymfudwr.

GAN D. AP G., AP HUW, FEDDYG.

HEFYD,

CAN YR YMFUDWR,

GAN EBEN FARDD.

CAERNARFON:

ARGRAFFWYD, CYHOEDDWYD, AC AR WERTH GAN H. HUMPHREYS, CASTLE SQUARE.

Figure 1.   Frontispiece from 'Gwlad yr Aur'.

Part 1

Historical Connections

The Welsh in Australian Historical Writing

Bob Reece

[Another version of this paper appears in Australian Studies, number 4, December 1990, pages 88 to 104; published by the British Australian Studies Association.]

With a name like mine, I might appear well placed to write about the Welsh in Australia. My paternal grandfather, Thomas Reece, was born near Swansea in about 1861 and made his way to South Australia in about 1881. According to family tradition, he ran away to sea and as there is no record of his arrival in the Adelaide shipping lists, he may well have jumped ship there. Working as a woodcutter in the Adelaide Hills, he met and married Susannah Gash, a labourer's daughter from the town of Gawler, in August 1882. After the birth of their first child, Thomas, in the following year, they moved to the old copper mining town of Kapunda and from there to Broken Hill in the remote north-western corner of New South Wales where mining for silver-lead began in 1884. Thomas worked as a labourer on the Broken Hill Proprietary Company's open-cut and then as surface foreman until lead dust affected his legs. He and Susannah had five more sons and three daughters and the studio group photograph taken of them in about 1911 is the very picture of a successful working class family (Figure 2). The Reeces were Methodists and talented musicians. Thomas himself played the fiddle and could sometimes be heard singing his way home on pay night. For a while before he died in October 1944 he spoke only Welsh and none of his family could understand him. I never knew him, but I do appear as a baby in a photograph of four generations of Reece males taken on the verandah of my grandfather's house in December 1940.

There is also a Welsh connection on my maternal side.   My grandmother, Catherine Murphy, was born at Cork in January 1876, the daughter of John Murphy and Margaret MacDonald.   However, the birth certificate reveals that Margaret was born on glebe land at Merthyr Tydfil in July 1845 and on 30 March 1851 the census taker recorded her as the eldest child of the family of Moses MacDonald, wheelwright, and Margaret née Keating. I cannot locate a record of their marriage in Britain and it seems likely that they were amongst the thousands of Irish people who came to work in newly industrialised South Wales before the onset of the Famine.   John Murphy, a successful plasterer, probably met Margaret MacDonald when he was employed making mosaic floors in one of the churches in South Wales and took her back to Cork.

That is almost all I know about my Welshness - and it is typical of Australians descended from Welsh people who came to Australia before the First World War. Working class emigrants did not usually keep in touch with their families at home and the Welsh connections of language and lore died with them.   The only Welsh voice in my childhood was that of the legendary Dr. A.E. Floyd, who spoke magically of music on the ABC's Children's Session in the 1940s. Although I like to think of myself as Welsh when addressed in Welsh in a north Wales pub on the way to the Holyhead ferry, or when hearing the roar of a Cardiff football crowd, I can just as easily persuade myself of my Irishness. My ethnicity, to use that much abused term, is not much more than a romantic fancy. Research into family history can provide some interesting information, but very little real sense of what it is to be of Welsh or Irish origin in Australia. Nevertheless, we named our son Owen in the hope that he might be interested in exploring the Celtic tradition more deeply.

This leads to the first point to be made about the Welsh in Australian historical writing: the interest in the subject is of very recent origin, arising partly from the growth of cultural nationalism in Wales itself and from multi-cultural consciousness in Australia. Assertion of their ethnic identity by relatively recent arrivals such as the Italians, Greeks, and Yugoslavs has created a situation in which the old majority of what used to be called British or Anglo-Celtic stock is being replaced by its components, the Scots, Irish, Welsh, Cornish and even the English: 'we are all ethnics now'.

For Australian historians, the recognition of diversity under the flag of British settlement was long overdue but the recent plethora of research into minority history also reflects the fact that the discipline has found a new growth area. It is also seen to be socially 'relevant' and worthy of financial support for its link to the ethnic vote. An inherent problem, however, is that it tends to be written in terms of the 'contribution' of the particular group concerned and is thus likely to be more celebratory that analytical. This tendency is clearly marked in the writing about Australia's first religious and political minority, the Catholic Irish, who were anxious to establish their credentials as nation-builders. [1] The fact that no such claims needed to be made by the Welsh (and indeed the Cornish) in Australia reflects their assimilation into the majority Anglo-Scottish Protestant population. They were not subjected to such discriminatory treatment and consequently did not see themselves as members of a minority. Closely identified with the mining industry, nonconformism and the struggle for social justice they tended to be subsumed under those historical categories.

Officialdom in Australia contributed to the virtual disappearance of the Welsh by perpetuating what Lewis Lloyd has called the 'for Wales, see England' syndrome. Separate statistics were seldom kept in Australia for people of Welsh origin who were generally subsumed under the category of 'English' or 'British', as they had been in Britain since the sixteenth century. Perhaps it is for this reason that they have not been recognised as a distinctive group in the standard studies of British emigration to Australia. [2] The first compilation of statistical data relating to them did not appear until 1987 with David Lucas' The Welsh, Irish, Scots and English in Australia. [3] Nevertheless, it has to be emphasised that by comparison with the Irish and the Scots, their numbers have always been small. Even in South Australia where they achieved one of their main concentrations they were vastly outnumbered by the Cornish.[4]

Deirdre Beddoe's Welsh Convict Women (1979) [5] is the only specific and detailed study of Welsh convicts, apart from some earlier work by Hugh J. Owen and E. Vaughan Jones of Merioneth. [6] Of the 179 women whose crimes Beddoe was able to trace, 115 had been involved in larceny of some kind and a further 30 in burglary (for which they were organised in female gangs). Many of the crimes took place in the newly-industrialised areas of South Wales, notably Merthyr Tydfil, although there were also some cases of animal theft in rural areas. All this suggested to Beddoe 'a more independent breed of women convicts than has usually been supposed'. [7] Her detailed study of 100 Welsh women sent to Van Diemen's Land revealed that 50% had been designated by the British authorities as prostitutes, many of them from Glamorgan which was a relatively urbanised county. However, prostitution was not a crime and it is clear from the case studies that the women regarded it as less important to their livelihood than larceny. More importantly, 35% had no previous conviction and 43% only one previous conviction, suggesting that women may have been unduly discriminated against by magistrates and judges anxious to redress the dramatic sexual imbalance of colonial society. Disappointingly, Beddoe tells us very little about how the women fared in Van Diemen's

Land, although this may be because they disappeared from official view (and from the records) once they obtained their pardon. It is interesting, however, that only 22 of the 100 ever married in the colony, suggesting to Beddoe that whatever they may have been in Wales, colonial conditions forced them into prostitution.

Lewis Lloyd's preliminary survey [8] indicates that there was a similar pattern of crime for the male convicts, apart from those political offenders who were transported for their part in the Merthyr and Rebecca riots, the Chartist assault on Newport and other incidents in the troubled 1830s and 1840s. Of these, the three Chartist leaders, John Frost, Zephaniah Williams and William Jones, who were convicted of high treason for their part in the Newport confrontation in 1839, have been adequately covered by David Williams' biography of John Frost [9]. However, interesting studies could also be made of the less known Rebeccaites such as John Hughes, whose letters to his family from Van Diemen's Land span an astonishing 56 years, and David Davies whose threnody composed in Carmarthen prison forms an unique part of convict literature. Altogether, the Welsh produced their fair share of political offenders, although these were distinguished more for their radicalism that their nationalism. This, together with their Protestant affiliation and small numbers, probably explains why, unlike the Irish, they did not form a distinctive group within the convict population. The only well-known Welsh convict, Joseph Bolitho Jones ('Moondyne Joe') achieved a kind of fame as Western Australia's only bushranger and most accomplished jail-breaker, although his exploits were anything but blood-thirsty. [10] 'Mad Dog' Morgan, as Lewis Lloyd reminds us, was almost certainly Irish. A broader picture of the Welsh convicts will doubtless emerge from the study now being made by Gwylon Phillip.

The first general book about the Welsh in Australia, Myfi Williams' Cymry Awstralia, [11] did not appear until 1983, although a longer version had been submitted to the Eisteddfod Genedlaethol Dyffryn Maelor in 1961. The wife of a Calvinist Methodist minister from Aberystwyth, Myfi Williams was mostly interested in William Meirion Evans and the history of Welsh religious and cultural activity in Australia, particularly in Victoria where it was first notable. Other chapters looked briefly at the Welsh in New South Wales, South Australia and Western Australia and a number of merchants and politicians. She made use of emigrant letters from the National Library of Wales and Welsh-language periodicals, including the two published in Victoria, but the fact that she wrote in Welsh meant that her book had no impact in Australia itself where there are now estimated to be no more than 1,000 Welsh speakers. [12] The same problem arises with one of the two articles about Welsh religious life in the colonies. [13]

The first major work did not appear until the Australian Bicentennial year of 1988 when the Gwynedd Archives and Museum Service published Lewis Lloyd's <u>Australians from Wales</u>. Although the book attempts a comprehensive coverage of the Welsh from Cook's voyages to post-World War Two Welsh emigration to Australia, its most original and strongest chapters are those dealing with Welsh maritime links with Australia from the 1840s (a largely forgotten phenomenon in Australia) and the experiences of Welsh miners on the Victorian goldfields in the 1850s. Lloyd's main focus is on the old counties which make up Gwynedd (Anglesey, Merioneth and Caernarfon) and it is the Gwynedd Archives which supplied most of the original sources that he consulted, together with contemporary newspapers such as the <u>Carnarvon and Denbigh Herald</u> which frequently published emigrants' letters. Between them, Gwynedd Archives and the National Library of Wales in Aberystwyth hold important collections of private letters [14] which pay tribute to the sober and industrious qualities of those who decided to try their luck in the Australian colonies rather than North America. Particularly vivid are the gold fields letters which Lloyd reproduces at some length. Apart from these, however, there is disappointingly little in this book about the Welsh in Australia. Lloyd is unable to say very much about the way in which the Welsh immigrants were absorbed into colonial (and later Australian) society. His collection of biographical sketches usefully brings together information from a range of Welsh and Australian sources but it is a pity that these are not listed, together with other material consulted, in a bibliography.

The Australian Bicentennial also produced a useful survey of the Welsh in Australia by A.F. Hughes in The Australian People: An Encyclopaedia [15] Hughes particular interest is the retention of language and culture and his doctoral thesis at the University of Adelaide should provide some interesting insights into that process. The late Elwyn Ashton was working on a book on the Welsh in Australia as a sequel to his book on New Zealand [16] and it is clear that comparisons with the United States would also be illuminating. Studies of the Welsh in North and South America are relatively numerous [17] but they do not appear to have been consulted to any extent by Lloyd or Hughes.

Although Welsh shipowners, captains and seamen were closely involved in carrying passengers and goods (notably, Welsh slates) to Australia and in the Australian coastal trade itself, Welsh free emigration there before 1851 was very limited and it is not yet clear why the Welsh did not respond more positively to the assisted passage scheme. The Colonial Land and Emigration Commissioners employed Welsh agents but Church of England clergymen were involved in the selection process and Lewis Lloyd has suggested that 'this may have put many Noncomformists off'. [18] Anglicans were certainly over-represented among the 788 Welsh assisted emigrants to Victoria in the 1850s.   Lloyd has also noted that, unlike the Irish, Welsh women were not prepared to emigrate to Australia as domestic servants and that this produced a disparity of the sexes within the Welsh colonial population which prompted 'mixed' marriages and thus assimilation. [19]

One of the first instances of Welsh working-group emigration to Australia, a phenomenon which survived until the 1920s, was the Australian Agricultural Company's importation of forty Welsh miners to its Newcastle colliery in 1840. [20] Emigration was further stimulated by the discovery of deposits of copper in South Australia where the Welsh population rose from 200 in 1846 to 900 by 1851. The discovery of gold in Victoria in 1851 also increased its Welsh population from 377 in that year to 6055 in 1861, peaking at 6614 in 1871. [21] So keen was the interest aroused by the gold discoveries that an emigrant's guidebook, Gwlad yr Aur (Land of Gold) was published in Welsh at Caernarfon in 1852 (Figure 1).

From 1861 onwards there are comparatively good statistics for the Welsh component of the total Australian population, in the form of place of birth. From these figures we can see that the Welsh total shot up from about 1,800 in 1851 to about 9,500 in 1861 and then increased slowly to 11,300 in 1881, 12,800 in 1901 (the year of Australian Federation), 13,600 in 1921 and 14,590 in 1945. After the decade of the 1850s the only dramatic rise took place in the 1960s, giving a total of 23,100 in 1971.

Figure 2.   Thomas and Susannah Reece and family, Broken Hill, ca. 1911.

To demonstrate how small the Welsh population in Australia was in relation to the other groups from the British Isles in the nineteenth century, in 1861 the 9,500 Welsh were set against 177,400 Irish, 97,200 Scots and 343,000 English. This relativity remained fairly constant for the subsequent hundred years until the 1960s by which time the number of Irish-born had dropped markedly. Thus in 1971 the 23,100 Welsh-born compared with 64,000 Irish-born and 840,000 English-born. Welsh emigration to Australia warrants attention but the only general study completed so far is an undergraduate thesis at the Flinders University of South Australia by Jennifer Newman in 1981. [22] Lewis Lloyd's preliminary study of working-group emigration (see Chapter Three) suggests that this is a rewarding theme to pursue.

South Australia's shipping registers between 1849 and 1867 enabled Newman to identify a total of 1243 Welsh immigrants, although this did not include indentured workers brought in by the Patent Copper Company as return cargo on copper ships and thus not counted by the immigration authorities. [23] The subsequent history of Welsh immigration to South Australia is obscured by the fact that assisted immigration was suspended by the colonial government between 1867 and 1873 and no records were thereafter kept of counties of origin. However, the South Australian census of 1881 revealed a Welsh-born population of 1,098 (1.8%), by contrast with 10,637 Scots (12.0%), 18,246 Irish (21.0%) and 57,540 English (65.0%). [24] Newman showed that the numerical representation of the Welsh in South

Australia was only half that in Britain and suggested that a major factor was the failure of South Australia's emigration agents to canvass Wales from the time of appointment in 1857. The one agent who did visit Wales, the Rev. John Thorne, reported enthusiastically o n Monmouthshire as a potential source, but the South Australian Government's 1877 Committee on Immigration recommended instead the north of Scotland, reflecting active lobbying by the colony's St. Andrew's Society. As Newman pointed out, 'there was no comparable pressure from a Welsh lobby to persuade the South Australian Government to include the Welsh in their immigration policy'. [25] There may well have been a similar pattern in the other colonies. The actual decline in the Welsh-born population in South Australia after 1881 can probably be accounted for by the end of mining at Kapunda and Burra and the gold rush in Western Australia. Many of the earlier gold miners had returned to Wales, which also suggests that for Welsh emigrants <u>hiraeth</u> was of greater significance than similar feelings were for the English, Scots and Irish.

Welsh emigration in the nineteenth century was stimulated by cultural as well as economic factors. Pressure on land in the marginal upland areas and fluctuations in the mining, smelting and tinplate industries certainly contributed to most of the exodus, but there were many who were repelled by the effects of industrialisation and anglicisation in South Wales and saw in emigration the opportunity to preserve their ancient but embattled culture in a new environment. This led to a number of communal experiments in the Americas, the most successful

being established in isolated Patagonia, although Forest Hill in Victoria

was apparently considered at one time. [26] It was this mixture of

motives which led to Australia replacing North America as the most

popular destination for Welsh emigrants in the period from 1852 to

1860. According to Newman,

> 'Gwlad yr Aur' ... challenges its people to arise from
> their apathy and misery and migrate to Australia. In
> the booklet the Welsh people are depicted as being
> trampled on by foreigners and their religion and
> language despised. They are censored for clinging to
> the bleak and barren hills, suffering indignities at the
> hands of the 'Season' [sic]. [27]

Certainly, the excerpt she provides indicates the almost messianic and

utopian tone of its appeal:

> Behold ... there is a country opening its arms to
> welcome us, its lands fruitful, its taxes low, its
> wages high and secure, its climate healthy, and its
> dust - GOLD. [28]

A slow-down in the South Wales coalfields encouraged emigration by

the mid-1860s and depression in copper-smelting in South Wales in the

1850 and 1860 resulted directly in the emigration of skilled workers to

South Australia. Later problems in the tin-plate and coal-mining

industries brought a further wave of emigration in the 1890s. Apart

from the 1840 experiment and the groups of workers brought out by

Zephaniah Williams to Launceston, by Lewis Thomas to Blackstone and by the Patent Copper Company to South Australia, Welsh emigration to Australia was largely unorganised and was not as strongly marked by the cultural messianism that produced the American experiments. Although the threat to Welsh culture in Australia led a Welsh-language journal in Victoria to tell its readers in 1867: *'Gorau po gyntaf y cyferion ein camrau tua Phatagonia'* (The sooner the better we aim ourselves towards Patagonia), a number of disillusioned Patagonian settlers later re-settled there. [29]

Welsh settlement in the Australian colonies in the nineteenth century, like Cornish settlement, was largely associated with mining development and the history of the Welsh in Australia is initially the history of mining centres: Kapunda, Burra and Wallaroo in South Australia; Blackstone in south-eastern Queensland; and a number of places in the Newcastle area north of Sydney. Ballarat, Bendigo, Maldon and other Victorian goldmining centres also attracted a number of Welsh although their concentration was not so obvious. Some idea of the Welshness of the smaller settlements can be seen from the fact that by the late 1840s Burra had its own Welsh quarter called Llwchr and streets called Llanelli, Llysnewydd and Penclawdd. [30] William Meirion Evans of Llanfrothen in Merionethshire is believed to have held the first religious service in Welsh in Australia at Burra in 1849.

The high point of Welsh cultural life in Australia was reached in Victoria in the 1860s with the Victorian National Eisteddfod which rotated amongst the principal towns of Melbourne, Ballarat and Castlemaine. In addition there were Cymanfaoedd Canu, some of which at Ballarat went on for several days and drew up to a thousand people. Various Cyfarfod Te, Gobeithlu, Seiat, Cyfarfod Pregethau and Cymdeithas Lenyddol were also reported in loving detail by Yr Australydd (1866-1871) and Yr Ymwelydd (1874-1876), the two Welsh-language journals published at Ballarat at the instigation of William Meirion Evans. Edited by Williams, these played a very important part not only as instruments of cultural preservation but as a forum for the colonial experiences of Welsh immigrants. By the mid-1870s, however, Yr Ymwelydd was bewailing the trend of the younger generation to abandon the language of their forefathers.

Evans was also responsible for the establishment in Victoria of the Welsh Calvinist connexion ('Methodists') whose chapels, together with those of the Wesleyan Methodists ('Wesleyans') and Independents (Congregationalists) have been the long-established focus of Welsh community life and identity. Nevertheless, sectarian differences continued to be significant and may help to explain defections to the Church of England.

Although the research has yet to be done, it does seem that most nineteenth century Welsh emigrants to Australia were working class people from the industrialised counties of Glamorganshire and Monmouthshire and that the three main occupational groups were

'agricultural servants, miners and smelters and domestic servants'. [31]
However, Lewis Lloyd suggests that many of the 1850s era non-
assisted emigrants were 'distinctly middle class': single young men and
heads of families who were fortune-seekers rather than settlers. [32]
Not surprisingly, it was the better-educated middle class adventurers
who left records of their experiences in the form of letters home and we
know little about the lives of industrial and farm workers. Joseph
Jenkins kept a fascinating account of his life as a (largely itinerant)
farm worker in Victoria in the 1870s and 1880s but he came from a
prosperous Cardiganshire farming background and his sojourn in
Australia was essentially an escape from an unsuccessful marriage.
Nevertheless his journals, edited by a relative as the Diary of a Welsh
Swagman (1975) [33] provide an uniquely Welsh view of late
nineteenth century colonial life, expressing Jenkins' growing radicalism
as he reflected on the treatment of workers by the big landowners and
the assistance given to them by all the instruments of state authority.
[34] Jenkins, who commenced writing at the age of 21 as a means of
improving his English, left a detailed record of rural life in Australia
from the point of view of an innovative and careful farmer who deplored
the rape of the environment and the rough and ready nature of colonial
society. Although he was sometimes thankful for the hospitality of
Welsh farmers and innkeepers whom he encountered in his travels, he
had no illusions about them and deplored the way in which some were
abandoning their language and culture. He was a voluntary exile who
felt no need to adapt or compromise beyond the exigencies of earning a

frugal living and continued to compose <u>englynion</u> on all manner of subjects for his private satisfaction. He regularly recited at the Ballarat and other eisteddfodau, while lamenting the corruption of the institution. In January 1877 he wrote:

> The eisteddfod at Ballarat on next St. David's Day is to be more of a concert where singing takes the place of composition. I do not consider that singing alone is of any advantage to keep up the language of the Ancient Britons. [35]

He regretted that the Welsh community in Maldon attended English churches, 'don't keep together like the other nationals do' and 'show great indifferernce to honouring their national day ...'. [36] All this he attributed to their desire to be fluent in English at the expense of Welsh. He also deplored the sectarian differences which prejudiced the unity the Welsh might otherwise have achieved:

> Four miles away there are three chapels belonging to different denominations. They are so close together that they are forever quarrelling. Mrs Lewis and her son walked to chapel to listen to a Welsh sermon, and I walked into the Bush to meet my God. [37]

However, while these differences may have existed initially where the Welsh settled in some numbers, the subsequent establishment of 'united service' churches suggests that where settlement was thin the Welsh language made unity possible.

By 1888 there were six times as many Welsh in the Newcastle area as in the rest of New South Wales [38] and their presence was reflected in such place names as Swansea, Cardiff, Aberdare, Neath and Rhondda. In no other part of Australia has Welsh immigration been so clearly marked on the political map and part of the explanation may be the continuing maritime contact which kept the language alive, supported the chapels and generally primed the cultural pump of a community which might otherwise have assimilated more quickly. Coalmining offered secure employment and subsequent immigration to the area was stimulated by the development of the iron and steel industries during World War One, a process in which the grandson of a Pembrokeshire immigrant, Essington Lewis, took a leading part as manager of Broken Hill Proprietary Ltd.

Unlike Irish emigration to Australia, which declined dramatically after 1913, Welsh emigration grew between the wars due to the downturn in the British coal industry. The modest flow resumed after 1945 and increased in the 1960s and 1970s, most of the immigrants coming from skilled backgrounds and settling in the industrialised areas north and south of Sydney and in South Australia. All this meant that the percentage of Welsh-born people in the Australian population, while low, has remained fairly constant at about 1.5% since 1891. However, their occupational distribution has altered over time, a 1984 study showing that English and Welsh males 'are more likely to be in professional, technical, managerial and administrative jobs than Scots or Irish'. [39]

The Welsh are well represented in the <u>Australian Dictionary of Biography</u> and some individuals such as William Meirion Evans, Lewis Thomas and Robert Roberts are included in the <u>Dictionary of Welsh Biography to 1940</u>. However, there is a need for further study of people like John Basson Humffray, [40] son of a master weaver from Newtown, Montgomeryshire, who gave up legal studies to try his luck at the Victorian goldfields. Arriving at Melbourne in September 1853, he made his way to Ballarat and soon became involved in the agitation there against the system of goldmining licences. As secretary of the Ballarat Reform League, he was deeply involved in the efforts to convey the diggers' grievances through constitutional channels to Governor Sir Charles Hotham whose reliance on the licences as a form of revenue had exacerbated an already volatile situation on the goldfields. Unlike most of the diggers, whose concerns were more immediate and material, Humffray saw the licence system, together with the squatters' monopoly of land in the colony and the conservative monopoly of political power in the new Victorian Parliament, as manifestations of an unrepresentative political system. Unlike Peter Lalor and some of the other members of the Reform League, Humffray was a believer in moral suasion and he parted company with the more militant and politically confrontationist miners after unsuccessfully attempting to persuade them to persist in constitutional action. Consequently, he was not involved in the Eureka Stockade but emerged soon afterwards to assume leadership of the constitutional campaign and was one of the more influential witnesses before the commission of inquiry into discontent on the goldfields.

Humffray was elected unopposed with Eureka leader Peter Lalor to represent Ballarat in the Legislative Council in 1855 and in the next year to the new Legislative Assembly under the manhood suffrage system for which he had so vigorously pressed. A notable orator, Humffray lent his powers to the radical democratic cause during the early part of his parliamentary career and was an energetic representative of mining and commercial interests in Ballarat, introducing a variety of legislation. He was Minister for Mines under the Heales government from November 1860 to November 1861 and chairman of the Royal Commission on Mining in 1863. However, he was defeated at the polls in the following year and after further defeats in 1871 and 1874 left politics. Like Lalor, Humffray was involved in mining speculation but did not do well and in the latter part of his life was plagued by financial problems. Like Lalor, too, he was seen by many to have betrayed the democratic caused by voting in support of pastoral leases and the dual system of education in Victoria. This was all the more striking because of his earlier espousal of radical democratic principles and his biographer will have the interesting task of explaining his growing conservatism. Peter Lalor at least had never claimed to be a democrat. Nevertheless, there is one anecdote which captures something of Humffray's mercurial and attractive personality during the events leading up to Eureka. After reading the Riot Act at Ballarat on 30 November 1854 and ordering a volley of shots over the heads of the diggers, Goldfields Commissioner Robert Rede galloped up to Humffray saying: 'See now the consequences of your agitation'. The Welshman quickly replied: 'No, but see the consequences of impolitic coercion'.

Another Welsh Chartist at Ballarat was Joseph Jones [41] who was also elected to the Victorian Legislative Council where he was distinguished for his free-trade and constitutionalist views. In South Australia the pioneer newspaper publisher Robert Thomas [42] certainly deserves a biographer, as does the Rev. John Lloyd, pillar of the Wallaroo community, and South Australia's first Labor premier, Thomas Price. [43] The Welsh were also well represented in retailing, David Jones continuing to be a household name long after the family company disappeared. Although there is a company history, the original David Jones of Llandeilo Fawr has not attracted a biographer. [44] A study of the influential Jones dynasty should reveal a good deal about the adaptability and social mobility of the Welsh in Australia.

There are excellent full-length biographies of two Welshmen who played a profoundly important role in Australian political life - Samuel Walker Griffith [45] the Queensland Liberal Premier who helped to end the South Sea Island labour trade, wrote the first draft of Australia's

Federal Constitution and became the first head of the High Court; and William Morris Hughes, [46] that 'fiery particle' who organised the Australian Labor Party into a disciplined political machine, galvanised the Australian and British war efforts during World War I, launched Australia on the international stage at the Paris Peace Conference, and helped to keep the Labor Party out of office nationally for two decades. There is also a biography of the geologist Sir Edgeworth David [47], whose tracing of the two Greta seams lead to the further developments of the Newcastle coalfields, and Geoffrey Blainey's study of the brilliant career of Essington Lewis. [48] The question to be asked, however, is just how Welsh were these men? Griffith was born at Merthyr Tydfil but only lived there for a year before moving to Portishead and Wiveliscombe and emigrating to Queensland at the age of ten in 1853. There is no indication that his parents spoke Welsh and he certainly had no acquaintance with the language. Returning briefly to Merthyr in 1866, he described it distastefully as 'a low-lying town amongst high green hills and immense heaps of refuse iron ore which makes it grimy and dirty exceedingly'. [49] Wales subsequently became for Griffith a romantic dream in which his own fancied descent from royal blood played no small part. Nevertheless, he named his large house on the Brisbane River 'Merthyr', just as the parents of Alfred Deakin, another founding father of Federation, named their Melbourne house 'Llanarth' after his mother's birthplace.

William Morris Hughes was born in London but lived and went to school for about five years at Llandudno after his mother's death before returning to London. Hughes did not record any reflections on his Welsh ancestry and heritage, although he may have imbibed something from his North Welsh carpenter father who certainly spoke Welsh and seems to have been a typical product of the nonconformist tradition. Hughes returned to Wales only once and it does not appear to have had any abiding interest for this man who in Australia became identified as the ultimate imperialist jingo during World War One. It seems somewhat fanciful for Hughes' biographer, L.F. Fitzhardinge, to say that 'Wales had given him his imagination, his eloquence and his gift of the biting phrase...' [50], unless we can believe that those years at Llandudno had a powerful formative effect. On a visit to England in 1907 Hughes recorded his admiration of Lloyd George's oratorical and other skills but did not attribute these to his Welshness any more than Lloyd George attributed Hughes' bull-terrier tenacity to the same factor. Neither Griffith nor Hughes seem to have taken any part, even in a token way, in the cultural life of Welsh immigrants in Australia.

A number of Australian literary figures were of Welsh descent: the dramatist George Essex Evans; the literary critic A.G. Stephens who edited the Bulletin's famous Red Page; Arthur Hoey Davis, better known as 'Steele Rudd' whose stories about life 'on our selection' have entertained generations of Australians; Ion Idriess whose tales of the outback did much to foster an Australian identity between the wars; and

Katherine Susannah Prichard whose novels of rural life in Western Australia were important essays in social realism. However, it would be difficult to say to what extent the world view of these writers was influenced by whatever 'Welshness' they can be said to have possessed. It is ironic that the greatest contribution of Australia to Welsh cultural life should be Robert Roberts' autobiographical Y Sgolor Mawr, which was written while he was in Australia but says nothing about his time there and is unknown there to all except the thousand or so Welsh-speaking Australians. On the other hand, in the 1950s and 1960s T.Harri Jones' poetry embraced both countries with its acerbic Celtic vision. [51]

As so little has been written, what should now be the priorities? This is a difficult question to answer because it depends on the different interests of historians and their readership. However, the Welsh in Australia raise a number of issues which might be addressed: their motives as emigrants; the organization of emigration; the significance of economic specialisation and the chapel for the retention of cultural identity; their role in the Australian labour movement and the quest for social reform; and finally, their influence on religious nonconformism. These might well be studied in the specific context of the more self-consciously Welsh mining communities in South Australia, New South Wales and Queensland. In particular, Wallaroo has considerable potential because of the relatively long life of the smelting industry from the 1860s until the 1920s and the coverage given to Welsh community affairs by the Wallaroo Times. And for the New South Wales communities there is the Welsh Australian newsletter produced in Sydney by Maldwyn and Blodwen Rees from 1935 until 1942. Indeed, the collection of their papers in the National Library, Canberra, is a major and as yet untapped source for the Welsh Australia-wide. [52]

Probably the most obvious area for general investigation is the involvement of Welsh workers in the Australian labour movement from the mid-nineteenth century until the Second World War. Historians such as Robin Gollan [53] have paid tribute to the British origins of unionism in Australian mines and to individual union leaders, but without pointing up the strong Welsh connection. And yet the history of mining form the 1840s and 1850s is inextricably tied up with Welsh immigrants and the skills and values they brought with them. I.E. Young has made a useful start on Welsh unionists in politics with his article on A.C. Willis and the Labor Party of New South Wales [54], but there is a great deal more to be done: not, of course, to glorify Wales and the Welsh but to establish the continuities which help to explain Australian history. Although the itinerant bush workers have been credited by Russel Ward and other Australian historians with responsibility for industrial unionism in Australia, Gollan rightly points to the radicalism which was born of the British working class tradition. Nor is it difficult to trace the Welsh influence: just to take one example, a Newport stonemason and Chartist, called James

Stephens, played an important part in the eight hour day movement in Victoria.[55]

One of the earliest industrial strikes in Australia was by the Wallaroo smelters from December 1864 to March 1865 in response to a cut in wages, inadequate medical facilities and poor management, the women taking as active a part as the men in their harassment of the manager [56]. In 1874 the formation of the Wallaroo branch of the Miners' Union sounded a militant note in its commitment to 'mutual protection against the capitalist classes' [57] at a time when the reigning industrial ideology was one of mutual dependence between labour and capital. A co-operative enterprise had been established at Wallaroo as early as 1867 and this, together with trade union activity, were facets of a strong chapel-based community whose other expressions were musical and literary.

If we cannot entirely escape from the notion of the contribution of the Welsh in Australian history, it is in the area of social values where they provided an important and influential example beyond their small numbers. The characteristicaly Welsh ethos of community cohesion and loyalty, social justice, public and private morality, and self-improvement through education and musical expression is one of the nobler reference-points inherited by Australian society.

Notes

1. See R.H.W. Reece, Writing About the Irish in Australia. Working paper No. 23. London: Australian Studies Centre, 1987.

2. R.T. Appleyard, British Emigration to Australia, Canberra: Australian National University Press, 1964; G. Sherington, Australia's Immigrants 1788-1978, Sydney: Allen and Unwin, 1980

3. D. Lucas, The Welsh, Irish, Scots and English in Australia: A Demographic Profile with Statistical Appendix, Canberra: Australian Institute of Multicultural Affairs, 1987.

4. Ibid. p.16.

5. D. Beddoe, Welsh Convict Women: A study of women transported from Wales to Australia, 1787-1852, Barry: Stewart Williams, 1979.

6. E. Vaughan Jones, 'Sheep Stealing at Llangelynin in 1792',Journal of the Merioneth Historical and Record Society, Vol. VII, pp. 384-403; H.J. Owen, Echoes of Old Merioneth, 1944 and From Merioneth to Botany Bay, Bala (Wales): R. Evans, 1952.

7. Beddoe, op. cit., p.70.

8. L. Lloyd, Australians from Wales, Gwynedd Archives, 1988, Chapter 2.

9. D. Williams, John Frost: A Study in Chartism, Cardiff: University of Wales Press, 1939.

10. See Australian Dictionary of Biography, Vol. IV, Melbourne: Melbourne University Press, 1972, p. 482.

11.   M. Williams, <u>Cymry Awstralia</u>, Llandybie: Christopher Davies, 1983.

12.   M. Clyne, <u>Multilingual Australia</u>, Melbourne: River Seine Publications, 1982, Table 9A, cited by Lucas, <u>op.cit.</u>, p. 43.

13.   E.G. Jones, 'Annibynwyr Cymrag Awstralia', <u>Y Cofiadur</u>, 26 March 1956, pp. 3-40; B. Owen, 'Bedyddwyr Cymreig Awstralia 1851-80', <u>Trafodion Cymdeithas Hanes Y Bedyddwyr</u>, 1960, pp. 42-50.

14.   See 'The Welsh in Australia: a Bibliography' by Ceris Gruffydd, at the end of this volume.

15.   A.F. Hughes, 'The Welsh', in J. Jupp, ed., <u>The Australian People: an Encyclopaedia of the Nation, its People and their Origins</u>, Sydney: Angus and Robertson, 1988, pp. 840-45.

16.   E.T. Ashton, <u>The Welsh in New Zealand</u>, Shoreham: E.T. Ashton, 1986.

17.   See, e.g., E.G. Hartmann, <u>Americans from Wales</u>, Boston: Christopher Publishing House, 1967. This book contains an extremely useful bibliography of the Welsh in the United States.

18.   Personal communication from Lewis Lloyd, 14 July 1989.

19.   <u>Ibid</u>

20.   J. Docherty, <u>Newcastle</u>, Sydney: Hale and Iremonger, 1983, pp. 14-16, cited by Lucas, <u>op. cit.</u>, p. 32.

21.   These and subsequent figures have been taken from Hughes, <u>op.cit.</u>, p.32.

22.   J. Newman, 'Emigration From Nineteenth Century Wales, With Particular Reference to South Australia', B.A. Honours thesis, Flinders University of South Australia, 1981.

23.   Ibid., p.43.

24.   Ibid., p.33.

25.   Ibid., p.13.

26.   Ibid., p.13.

27.   Ibid., p.12.   Newman has incorrectly rendered the Welsh word *saison*, meaning 'foreigner' (Saxon).

28.   Ibid., p.24.

29.   G. Williams, The Desert and the Dream: A Study of Welsh Colonization in Chubut, 1865-1915, Cardiff: University of Wales Press, 1975, p. 151.

30.   Newman, op. cit. , p. 42.

31.   Ibid., p.46.

32.   Lloyd, op. cit..

33.   J. Jenkins, The Diary of a Welsh Swagman. (Abridged and Annotated by William Evans), Melbourne: Sun Books, 1977. See also S. Knight, 'The Swagman from Trecefel', Planet: The Welsh Internationalist, 61 (Feb. March 1987), pp. 72-76.

34.   See Inga Clendinnen's review of the 1975 edition in Historical Studies, Vol. 17, No. 67 (October 1976), p. 237.

35.   Jenkins, op. cit., p. 65.

36.   Ibid., pp. 155, 173.

37.   Ibid., p.85.

38.   G. Davison et al, eds., Australians 1888, Sydney: Fairfax, Syme and Weldon, 1988, p. 35.

39.   Lucas, op. cit., p.65.

40.   See Australian Dictionary of Biography, Vol. 4, Melbourne: Melbourne University Press, 1972, pp. 444-5.

41.   Ibid., pp. 489-90.

42.   Ibid., Vol. 6, Melbourne: Melbourne University Press, 1976, pp. 263-5.

43.   Ibid., Vol. 11, Melbourne: Melbourne University Press, 1988, pp. 287-89.

44.   Times on Sunday (Sydney), 14 and 21 February 1988.

45.   R.B. Joyce, Samuel Walker Griffith, St. Lucia: University of Queensland Press, 1986.

46.   L.F. Fitzhardinge, William Morris Hughes: A Political Biography, Vol. 1, Sydney: Angus and Robertson, 1964.

47.   M. David, Professor David: The Life of Sir Edgeworth David, London: Edward Arnold, 1937.

48.   G. Blainey, The Steel Master: A Life of Essington Lewis, Melbourne: Macmillan, 1971.

49.   Cited by Joyce, op.cit., p. p.1.

50.   Fitzhardinge, op. cit., p. 17.

51.   J. Croft and D. Dale-Jones, eds., The Collected Poems of T. Harri Jones, Llandysul (Dyfed): Gomer Press, 1977.

52.   Maldwyn Rees Papers, National Library of Australia MS 6781. A useful guide has been prepared by Brigid Ryan.

53.   R. Gollan, The Coalminers of New South Wales: A History of the Union 1860-1960, Melbourne: Melbourne University Press, 1963.

54. I.E. Young, 'A.C. Willis, Welsh Noncomformist, and the Labor Party in New South Wales, 1911-33,' The Journal of Religious History, Vol. 2, No. 4 (December 1963), pp. 303-313.

55. See Australian Dictionary of Biography, Melbourne: Melbourne University Press, 1976, Vol. 6, pp. 194-95.

56. Newman, op. cit., pp. 55.

57. Cited by Newman, op. cit., p. 56.

Wales and Australia:
The Maritime Connection

Aled Eames

On Thursday morning, 22 July 1852, the full rigged ship *John Davies* weighed anchor in the Mersey and was towed to seaward, outward bound. According to John Roberts, an Anglesey man who was one of the 502 passengers and crew aboard the *John Davies*, there were many tearful faces as they watched the little steamer (with the pilot and Mr Davies, one of the *John Davies*'s owners, aboard) which had towed them outside the Bell Buoy, drawing away, whilst the crew busied themselves to trim sails to make the most of the somewhat contrary winds which they now experienced. Roberts kept a diary of the outward voyage which was subsequently published at Caernarfon [1], a favourable and pious account which may even have been subsidised and commissioned by the owners, the Davies family of Menai Bridge; an early example of the now familiar travel publicity brochure. The frequent references to religious services held aboard would no doubt have pleased both the Davies family, leaders of the Welsh Calvinistic Methodists, and would-be emigrants, among the increasing numbers of members of that denomination in North Wales in the mid- nineteenth century. [2]

Both the master, Richard Hughes, and the first mate, W.H. Owen, were Anglesey men, and although the crew list for this particular voyage is not available, it is likely that a fair number of the other members were from Caernarvonshire and Anglesey as this was the common practice aboard the early vessels belonging to the Davies family of Menai Bridge. John Davies, after whom the New Brunswick built ship had been named, had died in 1849 but not before he and his brothers, Robert and Richard, and their father, Richard Davies, a prosperous village shopkeeper at Llangefni in Anglesey, had established a highly profitable ship-owning venture based on the Atlantic trades. In the 1830s they had taken shares in a number of small vessels built in North Wales, intended for the coastal trades, particularly the export of slates from the Menai Straits to Liverpool and London to meet the increasing demands of urban growth and both public and domestic building. In the 1840s they had seen an opportunity to expand this interest by buying North American built vessels, increasingly available at Liverpool, which could be used to carry slates and emigrants to North America from the Menai Straits and Liverpool, returning with very full cargoes of timber. By 1852 they had purchased twenty two of these comparatively cheap North American built ships, engaged in the highly profitable Atlantic trades, manned by masters and crews who had therefore served a tough apprenticeship in the North Atlantic for nearly a decade, and ready to meet the challenge of the much longer voyages to Australia, the Far East, and the Pacific coasts of America. The discovery of Gold in California and Australia gave an extraordinary impetus to such trades. The *John Davies* was not the first of the Davies vessels to sail for Australia, for even before the gold-rush days, the *Eliza Caroline*, 831 tons, sailed on 31 December 1849 from Plymouth with 275 emigrants aboard, arriving Port Phillip 31 March 1850, in a highly successful voyage, without losing a single passenger. In 1850 the Davies vessels *Lord Stanley*, *Infanta*, and *Caroline* all sailed for Australia, to be followed in 1851 by the *Carleton*, *Oregon* and *Lord Stanley* and many more during the next few years, once gold-fever had increased the number of emigrants. Sadly the outward voyage of the *John Davies* as chronicled in Roberts' diary was not without its tragedies, for twenty seven of the four hundred and sixty six passengers died on passage, many of them young children. On 8 November 1852, one of the Welsh crew aloft sighted land and the following day the *John Davies* entered Portland Bay, with one hundred of the young people aboard singing the one hundredth Psalm, a symbolic gesture which obviously pleased the diarist from Anglesey, and, no doubt, the owners.

The voyages of the Davies vessels have been mentioned at the outset not only because they represent an obvious Welsh maritime link with Australia at the time of the great emigration, but also because service in the Davies vessels provided a spring board for the careers of several outstanding Welsh master mariners employed in the great Black Ball

Line ships of the 1860s and 1870s. Before giving some account of the contribution of these highly successful seamen, however, it is necessary to recall the dramatic development of ship-building and ship owning during the closing decades of the eighteenth century, activities which certainly increased significantly during the period from 1830 to 1880. The need for ships to transport the slates and copper of Gwynedd, and the coal of South Wales, particularly before the coming of the railways, led to the building of hundreds of small wooden ships along the coasts of Wales. In rural areas such as Anglesey, the Lleyn penisula and West Wales seafaring became a viable alternative occupation to agriculture, and a considerable fleet of both coastal and ocean-going ships was registered in the small ports of North and West Wales. By mid-century Welsh shipowners were also investing in a considerable number of that vast fleet which came from the ship-yards along the eastern coasts of North America, particularly from Quebec, New Brunswick, Nova Scotia and Prince Edward Island. A glance through the Parliamentary Papers containing the returns of shipping registered at the various ports of Britain for 1870, for example, confirm this. Obviously the great areas for shipping were centred around the Mersey and the Thames, but compared to a selection of other English ports the number or tonnage of vessels registered at the Welsh ports is comparatively high.

While recognising that the majority of these vessels were engaged in the Home, European or Atlantic trades, it is nevertheless not surprising that with this degree of involvement in maritime activities, Welsh

Table 1: Parliamentary Papers 1871, LXI [3]

Return of Total No. and tonnage of sailing and steam vessels of and above 50 tons remaining on Register 31. xii. 1870

PORTS	SAILING VESSELS LESS THAN OR EQUAL TO 50t.		SAILING VESSELS OVER 50t.		STEAM VESSELS LESS THAN OR EQUAL TO 50t.		STEAM VESSELS OVER 50t.	
	Vessels	Tons	Vessels	Tons	Vessels	Tons	Vessels	Tons
Aberystwyth	68	2835	267	35632	-	-	5	431
Barnstaple	54	1765	25	1991	2	39	-	-
Barrow	1	29	14	1605	1	14	4	1037
Beauman's	109	3470	159	14073	-	-	-	-
Bideford	52	1731	71	8593	-	-	-	-
Boston	52	1834	43	3464	2	28	1	75
Brixham	45	1782	84	12465	-	-	-	-
Caernarfon	134	4418	341	38547	2	43	2	226
Cardiff	33	882	56	21306	38	643	11	3204
Chester	40	1348	76	5789	2	59	9	2370
Dartmouth	99	3407	119	15766	5	150	1	108
Maryport	11	192	102	20230	4	99	-	-
Portsmouth	160	4091	119	14042	6	135	7	460
Swansea	22	615	179	46784	18	465	10	1932

ships and seamen inevitably found themselves in Australian ports in the age of sail, particularly before 1880 when the development of the triple expansion engine enabled steamers to compete efficiently, and eventually to replace sail on even the longest haul routes.

The extent of Welsh involvement in the early voyages to Australia was probably minimal. Dr. Lewis Lloyd in his Australians from Wales and Deirdre Beddoe in her Welsh Convict Women have shown that there were many men and women sentenced in Wales who were transported to Australia in the Convict ships. [4] There may well have been some Welshmen in the crews of these ships: as late as 1847 a young Caernarfon man wrote a letter home (which was subsequently published in the Caernarfon and Denbigh Herald) describing a voyage from Woolwich to Van Diemen's Land in a ship transporting female convicts. But the first fleet of 1787 and subsequent convict ships were for the most part from the ports of the South coast of England, and despite the name *Lady Penrhyn* it does not seem that this transport in the first fleet, or any of the others, had Welsh connections. There is some evidence that a Caernarfon ship-owner, John Owen, Ty Coch, had a vessel which transported "several hundred" Chartists from Milford Haven in the 1840s. [6] However, it was the discovery of gold in 1851 that undoubtedly re-created the great demand for shipping and it was a happy coincidence for Welsh shipowners like the Menai Bridge Davies family that they had by this time a fleet of ocean-going vessels large enough to be used as emigrant transport ships. Swansea with its

already established trade with Australia, particularly the copper trade of
South Australia, was another port favourably placed as far as suitable
ships were concerned, but the numbers of emigrants were small
compared with the great exodus through the port of Liverpool. Dr.
Lewis Lloyd has, however, extracted a number of accounts from both
Swansea and Australian newspapers relating to voyages made by such
Swansea vessels as the Appleton, Jenny Jones, Emperor of China,
Alpha and Catherine Jenkins in the 1840s. [7]

Even in the small ports of Caernarvonshire in the 1840s and 1850s a
few ships were built which were destined to be deployed in the
Australian trades. In 1848 at Pwllheli, Robert Evans, Gadlys, built the
ship rigged Ancient Briton, a vessel of some 400 tons, and therefore
much smaller than the North American built vessels of the Davies
family. The Ancient Briton was said to have fine lines and a
magnificent figurehead representing an ancient Briton in full armour
with his watchful dog at his feet. The Swansea Herald reported the
arrival at Swansea late in 1849 of the Ancient Briton with copper ore
from South Australia: her crew were said to be Welshmen, for she was
"manned entirely by members of the principality". Two years later she
was lost with all hands in the pirate infested waters of the China Seas.
A Porthmadog vessel, the Ann Melhuish, a 376 ton barque, built by
Henry Jones for Liverpool owners in 1849, had a longer lived
connection with Australia for she was eventually purchased by a
Captain David Williams who sailed for Australia in 1863. She was

later engaged in the Newcastle, New South Wales, coal trade, carrying coal regularly to Wellington, New Zealand and returning to Newcastle with timber and general cargo. The Williams brothers, said to be from Porthmadog, were among the pioneers of the Union Steamship Company of New Zealand, and at one time there was said to be a photograph of her in their offices. She was later used as a coal hulk in Albany, West Australia. [8]

The discovery of gold in Australia inevitably tempted Welsh shipbuilders and owners to provide vessels as they had in the earlier rush to California. At Porthmadog, Captain Richard Prichard who had commanded the brig Gomer on many voyages with slates and emigrants to North America in the 1830s and had since come ashore to manage the Cassons Bank in Lombard Street, Porthmadog, could not resist the temptation to put to sea again in 1852 in anticipation of the boom trades to Australia. On 4 May 1852 the "fine new coppered and copper-fastened Brig" North Wales, 259 tons, was launched from the building yard of Henry Jones at Boston Place, near the southern end of the Porthmadog embankment. Some weeks later the Caernarvon and Denbigh Herald carried an advertisement inviting intending emigrants to apply for berths aboard the North Wales which was "to sail early in the month of August Direct for Melbourne, Port Philip" from Porthmadog, under the command of "R. Prichard, Commander, whose name is well known in emigrating passengers from Wales to America" (Figure 3). Unfortunately no information regarding the voyage has been discovered but Captain Prichard is known to have died at sea off the coast of California in 1852, and the North Wales went subsequently into the South American guano trade. [9]

The large scale emigration of the next twenty years, however, depended upon the big North American built vessels sailing from Liverpool, and, as already noted, the Davies Ships were prominent in this trade in the fifties as well as in the lucrative guano trade of the west coast of South America. More detailed accounts of the Welsh involvement in the Liverpool - Australia sailing ships of the 1850 to 1880 period have been published in Dr. Lewis Lloyd's Australians from Wales and my Ventures in Sail: it must suffice to note that although the Welsh ships and seamen involved may have been comparatively few in the context of the fleet of ships and seamen of many nations engaged in the trades, there were some Welshmen who gained considerable reputations among their contemporaries. The appointment of Captain Thomas Williams in 1860 as marine superintendent of James Baines's Black Ball Line Ships had far-reaching consequences in this context. [10] Son of a ship's baker in Caernarfon, Thomas Williams had gone to sea as a boy in the slate schooners of the Menai Straits and Porthmadog, and had graduated to command the Davies vessels Olivia and Glenmonarch in the Australia, Far East and South America trades. His account of the voyage of the Glenmonarch from Liverpool to Melbourne in 1859 was published in the Traethodydd [11] and is a good example of a literary effort in Welsh by a self-educated master mariner. Baines was in the process of expanding his fleet of great American ships and Captain Thomas Williams was obviously in a key position both regarding advice on the purchase of suitable vessels, and the selection of masters and officers for the newly acquired vessels all destined for the Australia trade (Figure 4). It is, perhaps, not surprising that he chose several of his erstwhile colleagues in the Davies fleet, men whom he had known in many cases since their early days in the slate schooners, men who had then followed a similar pattern to his own deep-sea career. They had almost all come under the influence of John Towson, Chief Examiner of Masters and Mates for the Board of Trade at Liverpool, who like Mathew Maury, the American oceanographer, advocated the Great Circle route to Australia which almost halved the time taken by the earlier routes favoured by the Admiralty.

It is not surprising therefore to find that some of the best passages under sail were accomplished by masters appointed by Captain Thomas Williams to the Black Ball Ships, men like Captain William Williams, a native of the little village of Rhiw in South Caernarvonshire, master of the *Commodore Perry* and later owner of the *Light Brigade* and *Donald McKay*; Captain Henry Jones master of the *Lightning*, Captain Hugh Hughes of the *City of Sydney* and the *Flying Cloud*, Captain Richard Hughes of the *Royal Oak* and the *Whirlwind*, outstanding master mariners, all three of whom were brought up within a mile of each other on the Anglesey shores of the Menai Straits opposite

EMIGRATION
From Port Madoc to Australia
To Sail early in the month of August,
DIRECT FOR MELBOURNE, PORT
PHILIP,

THE fine new, Coppered, and Copper-fastened
Brig, 400 Tons, NORTH WALES, R. Prichard,
Commander, whose name is well-known in emigrating
passengers from Wales to America.

Accommodation for First and Second Cabin, or the
Intermediate, will be fitted up with every care for the
comfort of the Passengers, and the scale of provisions
will be liberal.

Early application will be necessary.

For particulars apply to Mr. R. PRICHARD, Marine
Terrace, Port Madoc.

Figure 3. Notice to emigrants in the Carnarvon and District Herald,
            1852 (Illustration by courtesy of the Gwynedd Archives and
            Museums Service).

Figure 4. One of the *Cambrian* vessels managed and owned by
            Thomas Williams and Company, Liverpool, regularly
            engaged in the Australia trade (Illustration by courtesy of the
            Gwynedd Archives and Museums Service).

Caernarfon; Captain Richard Richards, son of a ship's carpenter from Barmouth who became master of the *Vanguard, Great Victoria, Donald McKay* and *Thomas Stephens* all of them very fine vessels; Captain David Davies of Llangybi who became master of the *Empress of the Sea* (Figure 5), Captain Richard Jones, Caernarfon, master of the *City of Melbourne* and *Queen of the Colonies* and Captain Edward Ellis of Bangor, master of the *Naval Reserve.* Some of these masters became shipowners themselves with shares in many of the vessels of the Black Ball fleet and several acquired land in Australia as a result of their frequent visits. It is evident also that some of the Black Ball Line's Welsh officers subscribed generously towards the Welsh chapel at Williamstown, among them Captain Owen Griffith of the <u>Western Ocean</u> and Captain Richard Richards of the <u>Thomas Stephens</u>.

When James Baines and the Black Ball Line experienced financial difficulties in 1866 and 1867, a number of the Welsh master mariners, led by Captain Thomas Williams, the marine superintendent in Liverpool, and Captain William Williams who had a similar role for the company in London, persuaded a number of their fellow countrymen to invest in the purchase of several of the Black Ball Line vessels, which continued to sail, however, under the company's flag. [12] A number of these vessels' names appear in the lists of ships insured in the Pwllheli and Nefyn Mutual Marine InsuranceCompanies, and both Captain Thomas Williams and Captain William Williams attended the meetings of these societies frequently together with

Figure 5. *Empress of the Seas*, Captain David Davies of Pwllheli; one
         of the Black Ball Line vessels (Illustration by courtesy of
         the Gwynedd Archives and Museums Service).

William Roberts, the Liverpool Welsh ship chandler who had been associated with Baines and purchased shares in many Black Ball vessels. [13] There is little doubt but that the presence of these powerful personalities from the wider shipping world had an impact upon the development of the smaller scale local shipowners and that men who had served in these ships were able to make the most of opportunities in the schooner trades towards the end of the century.

A number of diaries kept by Welsh passengers to Australia in the age of sail have survived, tiny fragments of the remarkable saga of voyages which people of many nations and varied backgrounds experienced. Some of the diaries, housed in the National Library of Wales and the local Archive Offices will be, or have been, published and are important supplements to the accounts which appeared in local newspapers. One of the most interesting is a diary of Margaret Stephens, a young Caernarfon woman who sailed for Queensland in 1866 aboard the *Naval Reserve*, a Black Ball vessel built in Maine and commanded by Captain Edward Ellis of Bangor, whom Margaret Stephens described in glowing terms:

> The darker the night, the fiercer the gale, the more likely we are to find Capt. Ellis at his post on deck conducting the management of the ship in person. We have all experienced his kindness to us manifested in a number of ways. He has tried to make the ship as much like home as circumstances and means would permit.

She also paid tribute to the other officers, two of whom were also Welsh, as were several members of the crew, and she has lively descriptions of ship-board concerts in which she joined her fellow countrymen in singing Welsh songs. Her comments on her subsequent voyage in another Black Ball vessel to the Chinchas for guano are a valuable source of information regarding the appalling conditions at that unhealthy and remote location where so many Welsh mariners, together with seamen from America and Europe spent seemingly endless months awaiting the loading of their foul smelling cargos. [14] Inevitably the diarists evoke something of the boredom of the long passage to Australia, confined as they were to their quarters and limited deck space, but most telling are their incidental references to the routine hazards of almost every voyage, of icebergs and dangers from fire, oppressive heat in the Doldrums, bitingly cold weather in the monstrous seas of the mighty southern oceans.

It is only possible to make passing references to the toll taken by the sea. The most famous of the myriad ninteenth century wrecks, that of the *Royal Charter*, homeward bound for Liverpool from Australia, wrecked on the rocks near Moelfre, Anglesey in October 1859, certainly made an impression on Victorian Britain and a host of writers, from Dickens to Welsh ballad writers hawking their efforts around county fairs. And there is a Moelfre connection with one of the most gruesome stories of shipwreck, that of the *Cospatrick*, which went on fire in the Indian ocean in 1874 when outward bound for New Zealand.

Because of panic only eighty or so of the four hundred aboard managed to reach the boats when the *Cospatrick* was abandoned, and these "lucky" people died one after another in horrifying circumstances without food or drink in the open boats. Only three survived, and one of them was Thomas Lewis, an able seaman from Moelfre where he was known as Twm Penstryd. Long after the days of the great emigration movement, sailing ships continued to be lost on voyages to and from Australia: the loss of the *Primrose Hill* near Holyhead within hours of leaving Liverpool and the *Sierra Nevada* almost at the end of her voyage to Australia are but two of the well documented accounts. [15] Certainly one of the most dramatic stories of shipwrecks was that of the Black Ball ship *Netherby*, ninety-nine days out of London when she struck a reef off King Island, Tasmania on 14 July 1866. The superb small boat seamanship of Captain Owen Owens of Llangrannog and his two fellow Welsh officers, Edward Jones, the mate and John Parry, second mate, saved all three hundred and more passengers: John Parry's voyage in another small boat to the Victorian Coast to obtain help is again one of the stories of this wreck still remembered at King Island. [16]

That great American maritime historian, Samuel Eliot Morison wrote a worthy epitaph for the great ships built by Donald McKay and other yards in North America for James Baines' Black Ball Line:

> Never, in these United States, has the brain of man conceived, or the hand of man fashioned, so perfect a thing as the clipper ship. In her the long suppressed

artistic impulse of a practical, hard worked race burst into
flower. The *Flying Cloud* was our Rheims, the *Sovereign
of the Seas* our Parthenon, the *Lightning* our Amiens: but
they were monuments carved from snow. For a brief
moment of time they flashed their splendour around the
world, then disappeared with the sudden completeness of
the wild pigeon. One by one they sailed out of Boston, to
return no more.

It is highly unlikely that the Welsh masters who commanded them and

the Welsh crews who manned them had such a poetic concept of the

vessels, but even in the closing decades of the nineteenth century when

they had long since disappeared   J. Glyn Davies, then working as a

managing clerk in the Liverpool shipping office of Thomas Williams,

Liverpool recalled:

In 1892 when I entered the office of my old friend T.G.
Williams, I was plunged in the midst of Welsh ships and
Welsh seamen; and there were real old timers amongst
them, who had served on the Black Ball Line. The
founder of the firm, Captain Thomas Williams, had been
overlooker for the Black Ball Line, and when the owners
came to grief he bought up a number of the ships and
manned them with Welshmen. The pomp and
circumstance of the Black Ball Line was spoken of in
bated breath as something that had been, and would never
be again: great clipper ships manned like racing yachts,
with vivid tales of races home with new season teas, and
of marvellous passages to Melbourne Heads. [18]

The successful ventures in sail of the sixties and early seventies led to

the overproduction of both iron and wooden sailing ships, and many

small shipping companies, founded in the years of high optimism, had

foundered by the mid-eighties. A number of Liverpool-based Welsh

companies, however, continued to manage large sailing vessels which were employed as bulk carriers of coal from South Wales, guano from South America, wheat from San Francisco and timber from Portland, Oregon. But many of them also had to take general cargos to Australia, and New Zealand, thence with coal from Newcastle in New South Wales across the Pacific to the west coast of South America whence they returned with nitrates. Many of the young Welshmen who had served before the mast in the great North American wooden vessels of the sixties and seventies had now qualified as masters of the new iron and steel four masted barques and full rigged ships. Captain Thomas Williams, the former marine superintendent of the Black Ball Line, realised in the seventies that the future lay with more moderate sized iron vessels which could be used in the Australian trades. The *Cambrian Monarch*, first of the line he establised, was built by T.R. Oswald at Southampton to the designs of Hercules Linton, designer of the *Cutty Sark*, to the specifications of Captain Williams himself, and the vessel was supervised in building by Captain Anthony Enright, one of the most famous of the Black Ball Line masters. [19] Some account of the *Cambrian* ships has already been outlined elsewhere, together with that of their rivals, the Welsh *County* ships managed by William Thomas of Liverpool who as a young man from Anglesey had started work as a clerk in a Liverpool shipping office, the Welsh '*Shire*' vessels managed by the Davies family of Menai Bridge, the *Castles*, managed by Robert Thomas, Cricieth and Liverpool and the *Celtic* ships managed by R. Hughes Jones, Liverpool. [20] Together these ships represented a considerable fleet of sailing ships in the Australian long haul trades. Liverpool-based for the most part, these ships provided an admirable, if tough and poorly paid, training ground for many young Welshmen who were subsequently to have distinguished careers in steam. Ports such as Sydney, Melbourne and Newcastle, New South Wales, became familiar to boys from remote villages in North West Wales, as they did to their contemporaries from Norway, say, or the Åland Islands; peoples of the sea. Stories of "crimps" such as Jack Sullivan in Newcastle, New South Wales, became part of the folk-lore of Nefyn and Amlwch, and the yarns of how many of the Welsh boys had "jumped ship" and worked ashore in Australia, some never to return, feature widely in the memories of seamen of the age of sail.

No doubt some of these yarns have grown in the telling but there must have been many a young apprentice like the young R.I. Thomas from Caernarfon who wrote despairingly from aboard the *Cambrian Warrior* in the Victorian Dock, Melbourne, in November 1897, that he longed to give up the sea. The *Cambrian Warrior* had had an appalling passage out, and young Thomas wrote to his uncle in Caernarfon "I am sorry to tell you I do not like the sea" (Figure 6). He had already written to his father, Captain Henry Thomas (who as master of large sailing vessels knew the Australian and American ports and trades well) asking if he could give up the sea on his return, "if he will I am going to be an Ironmonger." But young Thomas never returned to Caernarfon as the *Cambrian Warrior* was subsequently lost with all hands. Long and stormy passages contributed to the number of desertions from the merchant sailing ships of many nations in Australian ports. One of the longest of these voyages was certainly that of the *Denbigh Castle* which sailed from Cardiff on 9 October 1908, and reached Fremantle in June 1909 having battled for many weeks in the vicinity of Cape Horn whilst attempting to reach Mollendo on the West Coast of South America. [21] The master of the *Denbigh Castle*, Captain Robert Evans, had decided to abandon his battle with the seas off Cape Horn and, by running down the easting, went round the world to reach Mollendo. The meagre food ration allowed to the crew according to Board of Trade regulations, had already been reduced drastically and they still had to endure a passage in the Roaring Forties before they reached their first port of call, Fremantle. The *Denbigh Castle* looked forlorn and battered as she entered Fremantle after some eight and a half months at sea. Small wonder that the crew were ready to desert at the first opportunity, but all they managed to do was to end up with terms of imprisonment in Fremantle. To replace them, all the master of the *Denbigh Castle* could obtain were unskilled men: "four of them are off a sheep farm and the other two keep chickens." [22] The *Denbigh Castle* eventually arrived in Mollendo over thirteen months since leaving Cardiff, and then, having discharged their cargo, they sailed for Loboo de Tierra for guano for Antwerp. Her homeward voyage took one hundred and thirty-five days. She was lost with all hands on her next voyage.

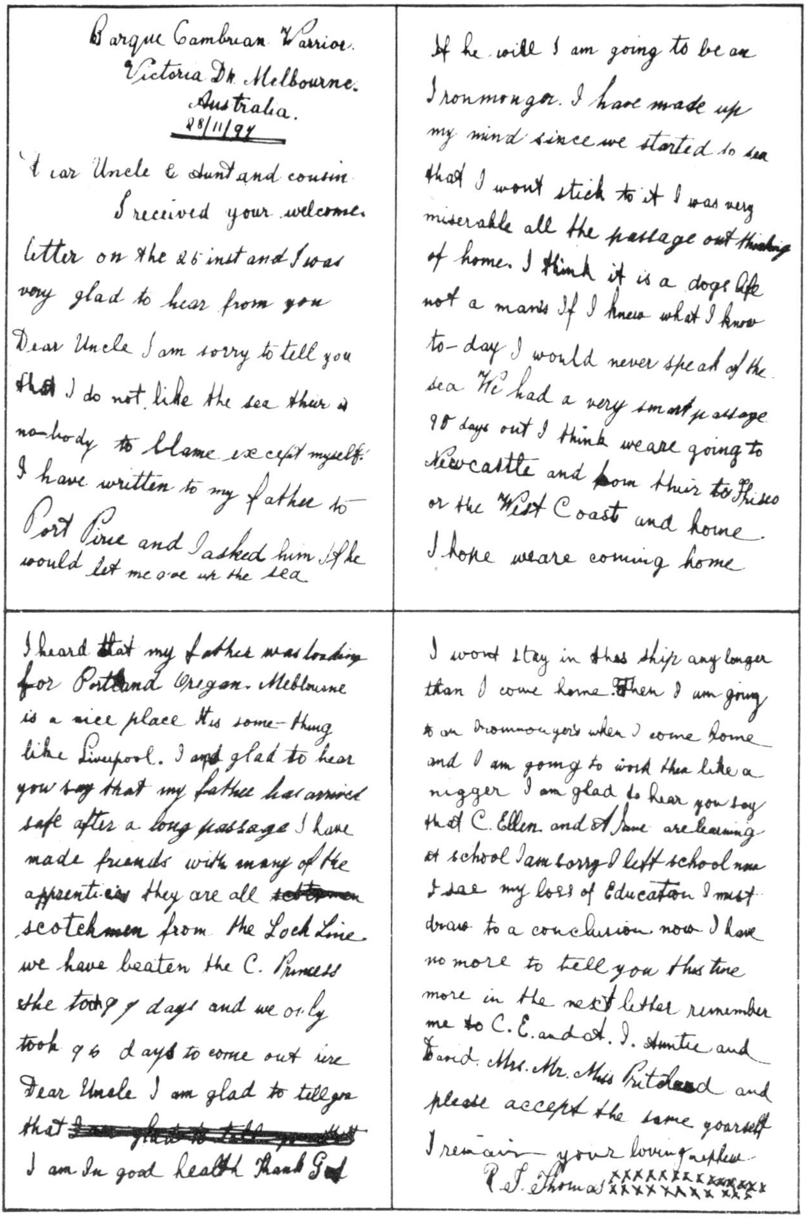

Figure 6.   A letter from a young boy, R.I. Thomas, to his uncle in
Caernarfon, describing his unhappy experience on a voyage
to Australia.

The sea so often had the last word. On 1 June 1889 the *County of Caernarvon*, a fine sailing ship owned by William Thomas, Liverpool, left Newcastle, New South Wales, with a cargo of coal for Valparaiso. Months later some wreckage was picked up on the New Zealand coast bearing her name, but nothing more was ever heard of Captain Robert Roberts of Nefyn, his fellow Welshmen and the Scandinavians who made up the crew. It was presumed she was "one of the vessels overwhelmed by the gale" which raged on the Australian coasts shortly after she left Newcastle. [23] When the *Carnarvon Castle* bound from Liverpool to Melbourne went on fire on January 31 1907, compelling the crew to take to the boats, she was some eight hundred and fifty miles from Cape Leeuwin, West Australia; Captain Evan Jones, the master, in one boat, and the mate in the other, sailed their open boats for twenty-four days with great skill, keeping up the spirit of the crew despite all the hardships. The mate's boat sailed into Fremantle on 24 February, and on the same day, two hundred miles to the south of Cape Naturaliste, the captain's boat made land. [24] In September 1910, the *Carnarvon Bay*, a steel sailing ship, 1932 tons, foundered off King Island, Bass Strait but the crew again saved themselves in their own boat. [25] Three ships with obvious Welsh connections which were lost in the Australian trade, another fragment in the much wider story of the maritime links between Wales and Australia.

Notes

1.   'Hanes Mordaith o Angylch y Ddaear, sef Mordaith y Llong,
      "John Davies" o Liverpool .... Ynghyda Hynodion Gwlad
      Australia, Gan Gymro o Fôn newydd ddychwelyd.' Caernarfon,
      1856.

2.   The shipping activities and background to the Davies family
      are discussed in A. Eames, <u>Ships and Seamen of Anglesey,</u>
      Anglesey Ant. Soc., 1973, 214-270; A. Eames, <u>Ventures in
      Sail</u>, Gwynedd Archives Service, Merseyside Maritime
      Museum, National Maritime Museum, Greenwich, 1987, 67-
      113.

3.   <u>Ventures in Sail</u>, 42. The table is extracted from lists in
      <u>Parliamentary Papers</u>, 1871, LXI.

4.   Lewis Lloyd, <u>Australians from Wales</u>, Gwynedd Archives
      Service, 1988: Deirdre Beddoe, <u>Welsh Convict Women</u>, 1979.

5.   The general background to the convict voyages is well
      discussed in Robert Hughes. <u>The Fatal Shore</u>, London, 1987.
      For emigration voyages, Don Charlwood, <u>The Long Farewell</u>,
      Penguin Australia, 1983.

6.   <u>Caernarvon and Denbigh Herald</u>, September 1902.

7.   <u>Australians from Wales</u> 77-89.

8.   E. Hughes and A. Eames, <u>Porthmadog ships</u>, (1975) 10,
      151-52.

9.   ibid, 33-35.

10.   There is a fuller account of the role of Captain Thomas
      Williams and the careers of the Black Ball Line masters in
      <u>Ventures in Sail</u>, 132-78.

11.   Y Traethodydd, 1860, xix, 291.

12.   There is an excellent account of the Black Ball fleet's fortunes in the standard work on James Baines and his associates. Michael Stammers, The Passage Makers, London, Teredo, 1978.

13.   Ventures in Sail 151-55.

14.   Margaret Stephens's diary was kindly brought to my attention by Miss E. Bellin, Wrexham; it is hoped to publish fuller extracts and her complete Welsh diary in my forthcoming Y Fordaith Bell, (Gwasg Gwynedd).

15.   Ships and Seamen of Anglesey, 353-4; Cymry A'r Mor/Maritime Wales 9. 136-46.

16.   Ventures in Sail, 147.

17.   S.E. Morison, The Maritime History of Massachusetts, 1783-1860, North Eastern University Press, Boston, Mass., 1980, 370-71.

18.   J. Glyn Davies, in his introduction to Cerddi Huw Puw (1923).

19.   Ventures in Sail 267-80; for details of Oswald's shipbuilding yard, Adrian B. Rance, Shipbuilding in Victorian Southampton ,Southampton, 1981.

20.   Ventures in Sail, 88-113; 205-64; Ships and Seamen of Anglesey, 248-70; 439-501.

21.   There is a good account of this voyage in Captain A. Bestic, Kicking Canvas (1957).

22.   Kicking Canvas, 128.

23.   Caernarvon and Denbigh Herald, 11 October, 1889.

24.   A full account of the loss of the Caernarvon Castle based on
        the survivors' reports appeared in World Wide Magazine,
        December 1932, 171-82.

25.   Cymru a'r Môr/Maritime Wales, 8, Alfred O. Jones; Gwynedd
        Archives, Caernarfon, XM/5774/36.

Some cases of working-group migration from Wales to Australia

Lewis W. Lloyd

Introduction

When compared with the English, Irish and Scots, relatively few people from Wales emigrated to the Australian colonies during the 19th century as non-assisted or assisted migrants. [1] Apart from such common disincentives as distance, expense and the taint of convictism, and the powerful counter-attractions of the United States, economic developments in Wales, most notably in the south-east and north-east, provided increasing employment at home for an expanding population as the British economic miracle advanced from the 1850s to the late 1870s. Furthermore, the population of Wales did not exceed 1,000,000 until the late 1830s; (1841: 1,068,547). Although Welsh people settled in all parts of Australia, the first concentration of Welsh settlers occurred in South Australia where the Welsh-born inhabitants recorded increased from 303 in 1846 to 879 in 1851. [2] The gold rushes to New South Wales and especially to Victoria from 1851-2 certainly encouraged increased emigration from Wales as from Britain and

Ireland generally. [3] The Welsh-born in Victoria numbered a modest 377 in 1851 and over 6,000 in 1861. Victoria's Welsh-born population peaked at 6,614 in 1871 [4] and thereafter, New South Wales and, to a lesser extent Queensland, attracted the majority of Welsh settlers, either directly from Wales or from Victoria, i.e. as employment in the gold mines contracted.

Apart from small Welsh 'colonies' in the major cities (Adelaide, Melbourne, Sydney, Brisbane, Hobart and Perth) and a scattering of individuals and families throughout the pastoral districts of Victoria, New South Wales and Queensland, immigrants from Wales tended to concentrate in the various mining centres, e.g. at Kapunda, Burra Burra and Moonta-Wallaroo (South Australia); at Ballarat (Victoria); in the coal mining districts of New South Wales (mainly at Newcastle in the north, and Lithgow-Cessnock in the western district); in Queensland at Charters Towers, a gold mining centre, and in the southern coal mining district of Ipswich-Blackstone, just a few miles to the west of Brisbane. Welsh chapels of various denominations (mainly Calvinistic Methodist, Baptist and Independent/Congregational) and 'Welsh United Service Churches' marked the Welsh presence in these and lesser centres of the extractive industries. Like the Cornish, who were much more numerous than their Welsh cousins in South Australia and in some parts of Victoria, the Welsh played a significant part in the mining and smelting industries of Australia in spite of their relatively small numbers overall.

Emigration to Australia in the 19th century was more closely regulated than the much greater emigration to the United States. Passengers Acts of the 1850s applied to non-assisted and assisted passengers to Australia, as they did, though they were less strictly enforced, to passengers (non-assisted) to the United States. From a relatively early stage, the provision of assisted passages was vital to the British and Irish settlement of the remote Australian colonies. Assisted emigrants were protected from the unscrupulous by stringent regulations of the Colonial Land and Emigration Commissioners, based in London, whilst agents of the Commissioners throughout Britain and Ireland were responsible for vetting and selecting suitable applicants. Mortality rates amongst assisted passengers in vessels chartered and regulated by the Commissioners were generally remarkably low. [5] When vessels arrived at their Australian destinations, they were closely inspected by the colonial authorities and officers, especially Surgeons Superintendent, were punished for infringements of the regulations. Yet, with regard to the selection of assisted emigrants, one can discern an underlying conflict of interest between the imperial and the colonial authorities. For their part, as an agency of the Imperial Government, the Emigration Commissioners were anxious to ship out to Australia, Canada and other British colonies, surplus labour, i.e. people who were surplus to current British requirements. Young Irish and Scots girls, especially orphans, were shipped out in large numbers as 'female domestic servants', whether the colonial authorities were likely to deem them suitable for such employment or not. [6] Although the Australian authorities required suitable young women as domestic servants (and as wives and mothers, variants of domestic servitude in many if not most cases), they also commonly requested various sorts of skilled/experienced men as rural workers (shepherds, stockmen, ploughmen, farm labourers, etc.), miners, smeltermen, building 'mechanics' (masons, bricklayers, carpenters, etc.) and so on. The supply of such key workers depended largely upon the condition of the labour market in Britain (and to a much lesser extend in post-Famine Ireland). There were times when the Commissioners and their agents were distinctly reluctant to encourage the emigration of skilled and experienced men and the men themselves were much less inclined to consider emigration, of course, when their prospects at home were good. This conflict of interest is reflected in the annual reports of the Immigration Agents of the Australian colonies and in other relevant colonial records to be found in the 'Parliamentary Papers' or 'Votes and Proceedings' of New South Wales, Victoria, Queensland and the other colonies. The conflict is also evident in debates on immigration which took place in the colonial legislatures. In addition, whereas assisted emigration could be controlled by judicious selection, non-assisted emigration could not. Provided a single man or the head of a family could secure the necessary passage money, individuals and families could emigrate even when they were likely to become charges upon the colonial authorities immediately or soon after disembarkation. In fact, many unskilled assisted passengers found themselves in a like situation upon arrival. Colonial employers and authorities were likewise indignant since they felt that they were footing the bill, and in more ways than one, with regard to assisted immigration in that the costs were met by sales of colonial ('Crown') lands. Some employers resorted to self-help by importing their own key workers.

Some employers in Australia, as in the United States, [7] arranged passages for key workers at their own expense but they generally preferred to obtain such workers at public expense, i.e. as assisted passengers consigned by Her Majesty's Emigration Commissioners. One important aspect of assisted emigration can be no more than touched upon here: evidence from New South Wales, in particular, indicates that certain colliery proprietors sought to manipulate the labour market to their own commercial advantage, at public expense, by having colliers sent out as assisted passengers either as strike-breakers or to force wage rates down by increasing the supply of miners in order to reduce the bargaining power of the existing and established workforce. The Government of New South Wales did not favour such tactics on the whole. [8]

We can now turn to the substance of this paper, to a more acceptable facet of colonial capitalism.

Three Cases of Working-Group Migration from Wales to Australia in the Nineteenth Century.

These examples are: the inducement of smeltermen from the Swansea-Neath district to emigrate to operate copper smelters in South Australia, circa 1860; Lewis Thomas's efforts to persuade Rhondda miners to work in his coal mines at Blackstone, near Ipswich, Queensland, circa 1880; and the attempt to boost production at the Bangor Slate Quarry, near Launceston, Tasmania, by the importation of Gwynedd quarrymen, in 1885. It should be noted, at the outset, that this paper is no more than a preliminary report of 'work in progress' since much detailed research remains to be done in each case.

Just before considering the above examples, brief reference should be made to another scheme when Zephaniah Williams, the convicted Chartist leader, sought, in 1853, to secure a number of key workers to operate his coal mine in Tasmania. Having been granted a ticket-of-leave, Williams found good coal measures in northern Tasmania, some 60 miles from Launceston. He was granted a conditional pardon in 1853 and, to work his coal mine, he commissioned his son, who was then at Blaina, Gwent, to procure and send him a workforce of 40 men - 33 colliers, 2 blacksmiths, 2 sawyers and an engineer. He sent tickets for their free passage to Tasmania and, having 2,600 acres of agricultural land at his disposal, Williams was also able to offer assisted passages to farmers, by the same vessel, at £7 10s. a head, or roughly half the steerage fare to Australia at the time. Little is presently known about this small 'colony' of Monmouthshire men in Tasmania. For his part, Zephaniah Williams encountered in 1855 the valuable Mersey coal measures some 25 miles from Launceston. This Tasmanian coal was soon exported to Hobart and Melbourne and proved to be, it is said, 'incomparably the best coal in the antipodes', at the time, at least. [9] Welsh colliers, however, generally looked to and went to New South Wales for employment from the 1850s onwards. As Professor Reece notes in the present volume (p.21), the Australian Agricultural Company had imported 40 Welsh colliers to Newcastle, N.S.W., as early as 1840.

1. Smeltermen from Swansea and Neath to South Australia, circa 1848-1860.

The discovery of rich copper ore in South Australia at Kapunda in 1843 and at Burra Burra in 1845 produced a surge of immigration of Cornish miners. Some Welsh copper miners joined them. When William Meirion Evans of Llanfrothen Parish, Meirioneth, arrived in 1849 to work at Burra there were sufficient Welsh people there to justify his delivering Welsh sermons - the first to be delivered in Australia, it is said. [10] By then, the Welsh miners had been joined by smeltermen (and their families) shipped out from Swansea and Neath in 1848 aboard the barque *Richardson* at the behest of the Patent Copper Co.

[11]   The *Richardson*, which arrived at Port Adelaide in October,
also carried the items needed for the construction of a copper smelting
works at Burra.   Lower grade ores were then smelted and refined
there between 1848 and 1870 whilst higher grade ores were commonly
shipped to Swansea for processing at Schneider and Co.'s works at
Spitty, near Bynea, the firm responsible for the construction of the
works at Burra.   The smelting works at Burra are now the subject of
a government-sponsored historical and archaeological survey under the
direction of Mr. David Banner and are said to constitute a site of 'world
importance within the field of industrial archaeology'. [12]

South Australia's copper ore, like that of Chile and Cuba, was shipped
to Swansea for smelting at Swansea and Neath, a district which was the
world's centre for the smelting of non-ferrous ores.   The copper ore
ships, such as the barque *Richardson*, commonly carried passengers
from Port Adelaide to Swansea and from Swansea to Port Adelaide.
[13]   However, the lure of gold in Victoria proved too much for
many copper miners (and the Burra smeltermen, perhaps) and in the
early 1850s mines lay idle for want of their miners.   The ore and
passenger trades were much reduced and never really recovered.
Copper mining was soon resumed and the mainly Cornish
entrepreneurs elected to establish additional smelters near the principal
mines.   The smeltermen were again recruited primarily in the
Swansea-Neath district.   It is said that 112 Welsh families settled in
the Kapunda, Burra and Wallaroo areas though no source is given for

this assertion. [14]   The smeltermen and their families certainly strengthened the Welsh element in these parts of South Australia. Even by the late 1840s Burra had a Welsh quarter called 'Llwchwr' and the town's street names included Llanelly (sic), Llys Newydd and Penclawdd. [15]   By 1859, the town possessed two Welsh chapels (Baptist and Independent/Congregational).   However, from a Welsh standpoint, a more distinctive and lasting Welsh community developed at Wallaroo, on Spencer's Gulf, from about 1860, a community, as Professor Reece points out (p.37), which was well recorded in the Wallaroo Times for over 60 years.

The Wallaroo smelters were built in 1861 to smelt the copper ore produced by Cornish miners at Moonta. As Oswald Pryor recorded in Australia's Little Cornwall, 'scores of men were brought from Swansea, Wales' to man these new smelters under the direction of Captain (the Cornish term for a mine manager) Lysson Jones, who had previously been in charge of the smelters at Kapunda. [16] According to Pryor, these workers and their families were 'fanatically Welsh' in that, some 40 years later, 'they were still using their native language, and their beloved pastor, the Rev. John Lloyd, was still preaching his sermons in Welsh in the Welsh Congregational church he had established'. John Lloyd, it seems, was a native of north Wales. [17] By 1863, there were 22 furnaces in operation at Wallaroo when the weekly output was between 35 and 40 tons of fine copper.   Commodore James Goodenough, who visited Wallaroo in 1875, described the area as 'the barest, driest spot conceivable'. [18] Wallaroo's dusty crooked streets were lined with neither gardens nor trees. Goodenough saw little drunkenness there but he did remark that, 'as in Wales' there was 'a good deal of keeping company of boys and girls, &c.' (what a pregnant '&c.'!). The smeltermen then worked 12-hour shifts and it is likely that the Rev. John Lloyd's Welsh sermons and the vibrant hymn-singing were the high points of the week for many of those who lived and worked in that isolated and barren place on the Spencer Gulf. (For industrial relations at Wallaroo, including one of the earliest industrial strikes in Australia, in 1864-1865, see pages 35-37).

Many questions arise with regard to these Wallaroo smeltermen and their families. How were their passages organised? How many were there? When did most of them leave the Swansea-Neath area to go to South Australia? [19] Passenger lists in Adelaide have yet to be closely and fully examined for the 1850s and the early 1860s. Additional information may be derived from letters written home and preserved by recipients (and their decendants). According to an obituary in Yr Ymwelydd, a Welsh monthly periodical published by William Meirion Evans at Ballarat in the 1870s, [20] William Thomas Evans, who died at Wallaroo on July 7 1875, aged 74, arrived in South Australia in about 1853 (some 22 years earlier). He later worked there as a smelterman, and although he had retired some years before, he must have been working at Wallaroo in his 60s. The Welsh certainly did not enjoy easy conditions at Wallaroo but they did create a viable Welsh community which spanned at least the first generation born in South Australia. The isolated location and specialised employment of Wallaroo were clearly important factors in this regard.

2. Welsh Coal Miners at Blackstone, near Ipswich, Queensland, circa 1880

The coal mines at Blackstone in southern Queensland were developed by Lewis Thomas (1832-1913) of Cardiganshire with the aid of a core workforce drawn from the Rhondda valleys. He had worked for some years in the iron ore and coal mines of South Wales. In July 1859, just a fortnight before he emigrated, he married Ann(e) Morris at Llandre, Cardiganshire. [21] His wife was to join him in Queensland in 1877, after 18 years of separation. Lewis Thomas sailed from London Aboard the ship *Essex* (776 tons), as a 'second class steerage passenger' to Melbourne in the company of the following Welshmen who, like Thomas himself, were described as mechanics: John Thomas (25), Edward Evans (28), William Powell (27), Thomas Powell (23) and Samuel Watkins (45). [22] He first mined for gold in Victoria for a year and a half, and arrived in Brisbane in April 1862 (the Colony of Queensland had been proclaimed in 1859). Lewis Thomas then worked as a coal miner at Redbank in Queensland and, in about 1865, he secured a contract to drive a tunnel, the 'Great Victorian Tunnel', for the Railway Department, through the Little Liverpool Range. After that, he worked as a coal prospector and located the 'Aberdare Seam' at Blackstone, near Ipswich.   He established a good market for the coal and, since experienced colliers were scarce in southern Queensland at the time, he contacted relatives in the Rhondda who arranged with miners, a number of whom may well have been natives of Cardiganshire, to emigrate to Queensland.   This resulted in a significant influx of Welsh miners to work at the Aberdare Colliery, Blackstone.   A letter written by a John Morris at Blackstone in January 1884 describes the voyage out and notes that some 80 Welshmen were then working in this pit. [23]   Owen Owens, a native of Anglesey, who was working at a roadstone quarry in the Blackstone area in August 1887, provided this description:

> There are coal mines for the most part in this place but I
> haven't worked in the coal yet.   They have sunk a
> shaft here recently.   There are a great many
> Welshmen here in this place.   The majority of
> Welshmen from round about like working the coal most
> in this place.   There is a fine Welsh chapel which was
> opened here about a year back - its a chapel for all
> denominations in a way but there is a bit of trouble here
> over denominations...   This part is a lot hotter than
> Victoria and Tasmania [Owens had worked at the
> Bangor Slate Quarry, near Launceston, in 1883]
> especially for working in the open air, which is what I
> am doing at present.   I am not intending [to remain]
> in this place for long... [24]

Like a number of his compatriots, Owen Owens was something of a 'rolling stone' in Australia.   He was killed at Waroonga Gold Mine, Lawler's District, Western Australia, on September 13, 1907. [25]

With the construction of the Ipswich-Brisbane Railway, Lewis Thomas opened the Dinmore Mine and had a branch line laid from the main line to serve his Aberdare Colliery.   Thomas arrived from Wales in July 1877.   The reunited couple prospered.   With their only daughter, the future Mrs. T.B. Cribb, they visited Wales and 'were tendered a welcome home on December 8, 1885, by the people of Blackstone'. At the ceremony, Lewis Thomas spoke of his early struggles.   As proof of his altered circumstances, the building of 'Brynhyfryd', a 'palatial residence' or 'castle', was commenced in 1886.   Located on a hill overlooking Blackstone, Brynhyfryd contained 30 rooms in its three storeys and its look-out tower afforded 'an uninterrupted view of 20 miles in several directions'. [26]   Thus the 'Coal King of Queensland' was installed in his mansion above his mines and the modest homes of his employees. In 1883, Lewis Thomas began his political career when he was returned as M.L.A. for Bundamba to the Queensland Legislative Assembly. He retained his seat until 1899 and in July 1902 he became a Member of the Legislative Council or 'Upper House' (M.L.C.) to become 'the Hon. Lewis Thomas'. It should be noted that, during the period from 1894 to 1904, the Aberdare Colliery at Blackstone was worked with the colliers on a co-operative basis as the Aberdare Co-operative Colliery Company. This was regarded in Australian mining circles as an important development and the practice was followed elsewhere in Australia.

Lewis Thomas also pioneered the Eisteddfodic movement in Queensland. He organised the first Blackstone Eisteddfod and his efforts in this as in other related matters were continued by his widow after his death in 1913. The Hon. Lewis Thomas's funeral in 1913 was numerously attended. Some 40 members of the Blackstone Cambrian Choir marched in front of the hearse. Thomas had been a staunch member of the Congregational Church in Ipswich and Blackstone, and of the United Service Welsh Church at Blackstone in which his brother, Thomas Thomas, had played a prominent part for many years. [27] The Rev. W.A. Lewis conducted a Welsh service at Brynhyfryd and the burial service at Ipswich Cemetery was read in Welsh, 'after which the Welsh citizens sang a favourite hymn of the deceased in their own language'. Some 70 members of the Blackstone Cambrian Choir also sang at the ceremony. Mrs. Thomas continued her husband's patronage. She was patroness of Blackstone's Cambrian Choir for over 20 years and she supported the Queensland Eisteddfod financially and in other ways. She died in 1929, aged 93, when Dr. Luther Morris of Gympie, the President of the Queensland Eisteddfod Council, said:

> Whilst the Eisteddfod movement continues to function and prosper the names of the Hon. Lewis and Mrs. Thomas, and the memories of their presence amongst us will be lastingly cherished. Eisteddfodau in Queensland to-day stand as a monument to their devotion in giving expression to the fine ideals emanating from the land of their birth.

Alfred Nicholas of Pembrokeshire, who emigrated to Western Australia in 1908, found work hard to come by so he and a Welsh mate made their way to Gippsland, Victoria, and thence to Blackstone:

> "Slackness of trade forced us to leave the State (Western Australia) and after a few months work in Gippsland Victoria we decided to try our luck in Queensland. We made for Blackstone and what a surprise, a group of boys playing marbles all speaking Welsh. There we attended the Welsh Chapel and the Sunday School was all Welsh. We did not stay long there as the wages were too low..." [28]

Nicholas had noted that at Collie in Western Australia coal miners were paid 13s. 11d. per shift. The miners at Blackstone were certainly receiving less than that.

Reports on Blackstone (& District) in The Welsh Australian newsletter in the late 1930s indicate that the area retained its Welsh character. In February 1938, Ceridwen Parry noted the passing of 'the Welsh community's oldest friend in Mr. J.L. Edwards of "Penybryn", formerly of Talybont, Cardiganshire, at the age of 77'. He had married Ann Morris of Garnant and was survived by four daughters and three sons. His son, Mr. L.D. Edwards, M.A., was then Minister of Education for Queensland. [29] In October 1938, Maldwyn and Blodwen Rees, the Sydney-based editors of The Welsh Australian, reported on their recent visit to the Ipswich-Blackstone district. [30] There they met Mr. D.L. Lewis, Australian-born Vice-President of the Blackstone St. David's Society, who had compiled, a few years before, a history of the Blackstone Welsh Church 'on the occasion of its Jubilee'. His parents

were from Ferndale in the Rhondda. In the same edition of the
newsletter, it was reported that a 'special Welsh Service' had been held
on October 9 at the Blackstone United Welsh Church and that it had
been 'largely attended by the Cymry of the Booval, Silkstone,
Blackstone and Ipswich'. These were, however, the twilight years of
this Welsh community.

Today, some vestiges of Welshness live on in the area, for example, in
such place-names as Ebbw Vale, Dinmore and Aberdare, and, of
course, in the names of many inhabitants: for example, Sir Llewellyn
Edwards, who organised Brisbane's hugely successful 'World Expo 88'
in 1988. Coal mining in the district is now much reduced but the
Rhondda Colliery, Blackstone, survives. The area known as the
Booval presents a run-down appearance. Many of its weatherboard
houses, where many colliers once lived, stand empty whilst others are
used as storehouses. It is a familiar story the world over. The city
centre of Ipswich, on the other hand, has been brashly modernised and
appears quite prosperous though many citizens dread the prospect of
their city becoming a western suburb of a sprawling greater Brisbane.
Such is 'the curse of bigness'. [31]

3. Gwynedd Slate Quarrymen at Bangor Quarry, near Launceston, Tasmania, circa 1885.

The evidence in this case is much more limited than in either of the two cases already considered. The origins of the Bangor Slate Quarry are not known. However, a letter written by one Daniel Jones in Portland, Victoria, in 1857, and sent to a friend, William Griffith, at Caernarfon, noted that a slate quarry had been opened recently in Tasmania. [32] The slates were said to be 'good and obtainable of any size and in any quantity'. Although Jones did not specify this quarry's location within Tasmania, it may well have been the Bangor Quarry or on the site of the quarry later given that name by Gwynedd quarrymen.

The existence of the Bangor Quarry was publicised in an advertisement for skilled quarrymen which appeared in the North Wales Chronicle of Bangor on March 14 1885. An expansion programme was underway. The advertisement, in Welsh and English, stated that the Bangor Slate Quarry, near Launceston, Tasmania, an indication that it was already a going concern, required 100 'Splitters and Rockmen' *(Holltwyr a Chreigwyr)*. The wages offered were 7s. 6d. for an eight-hour day or 7s. 6d. 'for Countess Slates". Married men with small families were preferred. 'Intending Emigrants, of the above classes', were offered free passages, but those who paid the full passage money were to be entitled to a 'FREE GRANT OF LAND'. Particulars of the land grants could be obtained from the Tasmanian Emigration Department, $79^1/_2$

Gracechurch Street, London, E.C., and details of the free passages from G. Griffiths, Esq., of Criccieth, Caernarfonshire. The response to this advertisment is presently unknown, but the slate industry of Gwynedd, the basis of the region's economy, was in recession at this time and many quarrymen were then emigrating to the United States and Canada. [33] Distant Tasmania, which never attracted many emigrants from Wales, [34] was probably a much less attractive destination. Further research, particularly in Tasmania, is clearly needed here.

Although these three cases of working-group migration occurred in the 19th century, it is worth noting, in conclusion, that a number of quarrymen left Blaenau Ffestiniog in 1926-7 to work at a slate quarry at Goulburn, New South Wales. [35] There are several references to these 'Goulburn boys' in The Welsh Australian newsletter in the late 1930s. For example, this report was published in the newsletter of January 22 1938 No. 30:

> The arrival in Sydney of Mr. Robert 'Dai' Owen (Robert David Owen) formerly of Ffestiniog and Goulburn, after an absence of nine years in Tasmania and Victoria, resulted in a reunion of the "Goulburn boys" in the Welsh Church (Chalmers Street, Sydney). Mr. Bob Owen is the possessor of a fine tenor voice and is in the cast of 'Balalaika' which is now being played to crowded audiences in the Theatre Royal. Among the 'boys' who foregathered were Messrs. Iorwerth Jones, 'Bob' Griffiths, Bill Davies, and R.'Wmphre' (Humphrey) Jones of Goulburn.

It was noted that several of the 'boys' were still in their teens when they emigrated to Australia to work at Goulburn and that 'although most of them are scattered throughout the world, the friendships have continued'. Some remained in Goulburn. In a letter to Mr. Maldwyn Rees ('Dyffryn Amman') and his wife Blodwen ('Siaradus') as editors of The Welsh Australian, dated November 16 1938, Mrs. Mary Stone (née Evans) of 'Four Winds', Fitzroy Street, Goulburn, who had been a student at University College, Cardiff, from 1922 to 1927, said:

> I'm seriously contemplating a Welsh Society in Goulburn. What do you think of the idea? I have only been here a short while, but I'm beginning to discover the Cymry here. [36]

Perhaps other examples of working-group migrations from Wales to Australia during the troubled inter-war years will come to light.

Notes

1. See, for example, in the Victorian Public Record Office ('Information Victoria'), 318 Little Bourke St., Melbourne, VPRS 3502: Assisted Passengers from U.K. Ports, 1839-1871; and VPRS 3501: Unassisted passengers from U.K. Ports, 1852-1923. During the 1850s, less than 800 assisted Passengers from Wales (including Monmouthshire) are listed, though more emigrated without assistance. The reverse was true of the other U.K. nationalities. This will be addressed in another paper.   In the meantime, see Lewis Lloyd, 'A Report on my recent researches in Australia', <u>Cymru a'r Môr/Maritime Wales</u>, No. 12, 1989, pp.7-26, at pp.12-17; cf. Professor Reece, pp.20-21.

2. <u>Australians: Historical Statistics,</u> Ed. Wray Vamplew, Fairfax, Syme and Weldon Associates, IEO 7581. In 1856, the Welsh-born numbered 1086 in a U.K. total of 60,959. Natives of Monmouthshire were probably excluded from the Welsh-born figure.

3. Victoria: Votes and Proceedings (Legislative Council) Session 1854-55, A 8 Report of the Immigration Agent for 1851-53.

4. A.F. Hughes, 'WELSH', in <u>The Australian People</u> (Canberra, 1988), General Editor - James Jupp, pp. 840-845, at p. 842. See also D. Lucas, <u>The Welsh, Irish, Scots and English</u>: A Demographic Profile with Statistical Appendix (Canberra, 1987), an informative and most readable study.

5. Vict.: V & P(L.C.) Sess. 1859-60, Vol. III, No.6: Report of the Immigration Agent for 1858. The average mortality rates for assisted passengers were: 1852, 5.5%; 1853, 3.6%; 1854, 1.47%; 1855, 1.45%; 1856, 1.7%; 1857, 0.8%; and 1858, 1.2%.

6. E.g. N.S.W.: V & P (Legislative Assembly) Part 2, 1856: Immigration Agent's Report, 1855, para. 89, where it was noted: 'the feeling of the Colony was much against the

introduction of rough Irish girls'. However, such was the demand, few remained unhired for long.

7.   Lewis Lloyd, Australians from Wales (Caernarfon: Gwynedd Archives & Museums Service, 1988), p.201, for the emigration of a group of coal miners, 'artificiers' and their families from Llanelli in 1853 to work for the West Columbian Mining Company on the banks of the Ohio.

8.   N.S.W.: V & P (L.A.) Sess. 1861-62, Vol. 2, p. 819, et. seq. , re. scheme to import nearly 500 miners and others by the Australian Agricultural Co., the principal colliery owner of the Newcastle district; and N.S.W.: V & P (L.A.) Sess. 1879-80, Vol. 5, p. 721 et seq.: Report of the Select Committee on Assisted Immigration (with Evidence).

9.   Lewis Lloyd, op.cit., p.53; and the Merlin Nov. 4 1853 (for a copy of the letter).

10.   Lewis Lloyd, op. cit., p. 216; and The Dictionary of Welsh Biography for entry on W.M. Evans by Bob Owen, Croesor.

11.   'Welsh Copper-Smelting Works in Australia', South West Wales Industrial Archaeology Society Bulletin, No.51, May 1990, pp.7-8.   A note based on information provided by David Bannear.   I am most grateful to Ceris Gruffudd of the National Library of Wales for sending me a copy of this note.
The Patent Copper Co. was succeeded in 1851 at Burra by the English & Australian Copper Co.   See also, in the present volume, pages 21-22, citing Jennifer Newman, re. Welsh immigrants in South Australia.

12.   Ibid. p.7.   This was the cargo of the *Richardson* in 1848: 48,100 fire-bricks, 40 tons fire-clay, 300 furnace slabs, 200 furnace doors, 120 furnace bearers, 10 tons of sand (probably a special sand used for repairing the lining of copper furnaces in the Swansea-Neath area), 45 tons castings, 12 tons wrought iron in bars, 1 ton shovels and other tools, $1^1/_2$ tons pig and sheet lead, 30 barrows, 4 dozen brooms, 6 cases containing apparatus for laboratory, 1 case scale-beams, 1 case a copying

machine, 1 cask crucibles, ironmongery and other implements.

13.   Lewis Lloyd, op.cit., pp.77-89, The Port Adelaide-Swansea Connexion, 1846-1851.

14.   Ms 6781 'Maldwyn Rees Collection' (National Library of Australia, Canberra), Box/Series 3, Folder 15 - notes on Welsh settlers in Australia compiled by Mrs. Rees.

15.   A.F. Hughes, op. cit., p. 842.

16.   O. Pryor, Australia's Little Cornwall. Adelaide: Rigby Ltd., 1962, p. 96.

17.   Ms 6781 (N.L.A., Canberra) Box 3, Folder 15, Mrs. Rees.

18.   Cited by Geoffrey Blainey, The Rush That Never Ended, (Melbourne, 1963) p. 118.

19.   VPRS 4319: Index to Inwards Assisted Immigrant Lists (to South Australia) 1845-1886, in the Victorian P.R.O., is helpful in this regard, but no substitute for the Lists themselves in Adelaide, of course.   But, if they were indentured workers, like those aboard the *Richardson* in 1948, Professor Reece (Chapter One) indicates they would not have been listed as immigrants in the normal way.

20.   Yr Ymwelydd Awst (August) 16 1875 Rhif II Cyf. 1, t. 239. W. T. Evans was a native of Swansea, Yr Ymwelydd (The Visitor) published from 1874-76.   Yr Australydd (The Australian), which also contains references to Wallaroo, appeared monthly from 1866 to 1872.   According to Professor Reece (Chapter One) the Wallaroo Times provided full coverage of the Welsh community from the 1860s to the 1920s.

21.   Lewis Lloyd, op. cit., pp. 239-241 (and the sources cited at p. 241).

22.   VPRS 3501 Fiche No. 169 *Essex* Oct./Nov. 1859. The *Essex*, commanded by Geo. H. Bawn, carried 75 passengers on this occasion. As in all these unassisted passenger lists, the Welsh were classified as 'English'.

23.   National Library of Wales Ms 3194C (Welsh-Australian materials).

24.   Letter from O. Owens at Bundamba (some 2 miles east of Ipswich) in H.S. Chapman, 'Welsh Emigration to Australia: A Case Study, Gwreiddiau Gwynedd Roots (Newsletter of the Gwynedd Family History Society), Spring 1985, No.8, pp.2-9, at p.4.

25.   Ibid., P.6.   See n.33 below for O. Owens at the Bangor Slate Quarry, near Launceston, Tasmania.

26.   'The Brynhyfryd Story' by N.A. Perry, N.L.W. Ex 4999.

27.   According to a brief biography of Thomas Thomas by his daughter Miss M. Thomas in Blackstone. Ms 6781 (N.L.A., Canberra). Folder 12. He emigrated in 1885 and died in Brisbane in 1909, aged 66.

28.   Ms 6782 Book 3 Folder 16.

29.   The Welsh Australian Feb. 26 1938 (Ms 6781 Folder 19).

30.   Ibid. Oct. 28 1938 No. 39 (Ms 6781 Box 2).

31.   I visited the Ipswich-Blackstone district in September 1988 and spent four days there.   Dr. Ross Johnston of the University of Queensland, St. Lucia, Brisbane, was in Wales in 1990 studying emigration from Wales to Queensland in the late 19th Century.

32.   Carnarvon and Denbigh Herald Feb. 8 1858,

33.   H.S. Chapman, op.cit., p.4: letter from Owen Jones of Anglesey to his sister in wales dated, at Ballarat, August 13 1883, giving the address of his nephew Owen Owens -

'Bangor Slate Quarry, Turners Marsh, near Launceston, Tasmania', i.e. nearly 2 years before the advertisement in the North Wales Chronicle.

34.   Australians: Historical Statistics, Ed. Wray Vamplew, IEO 82-89: Welsh-born inhabitants of Tasmania in 1861 numbered 565 out of a Welsh-born total for Australian of 9,467; IEO 90-98: the figures were 321 and 12,792 in 1901; IEO 109-118: in 1981 the figures were 561 (Tasmania) and 24,868 (Australia). Natives of Monmouthshre (Gwent) may have been counted as 'English' in 1861 and 1901. Monmouthshire was regarded as a midland county of England.

35.   Oral evidence of Mr. Richard Williams of Harlech, who remembers as a boy in his native Blaenau Ffestiniog the large crowd which assembled to bid farewell to these emigrants. It appears that they were engaged as a group to work at Goulburn. They were joined by some Caernarfonshire men. Also, oral evidence of Mr. Owain Gwynedd Lloyd of Blaenau Ffestiniog.

36.   Ms 6781 (N.L.A., Canberra) Box 1 Folder 2. Mr. Maldwyn Rees was then, inter alia, Vice-President of Cymdeithas Cymraeg, the Sydney Welsh Society.

Part 2

Cultural Connections and Parallels

Sinking into the Landscape - Notes on Anglo-Welsh Literature and Australia

Ned Thomas

Any history of Welsh/Australian literary relations would have to take account of numerous and disparate kinds of connection. It would have something to say about Joseph Jenkins who at the age of 51 left his wife and seven children and a farm called Trecefel, near Tregaron in Ceredigion, to be a swagman whose diary of visits to farms in Australia (some of them Welsh-owned) is of historical interest certainly, and of some literary interest too. [1] In the other direction there is the poet Les Murray's interest in cynghanedd, that is to say, the alliterative craft of the Welsh strict metres, and in the whole tradition of Welsh praise poetry. [2] Yet again, one of the most obscure poems in modern Welsh, 'O Bridd' by Waldo Williams [3] (Wales's most breathtaking poet of this century, not forgetting Dylan Thomas) is rendered that bit less obscure when read in the context of the nineteenth century Australian Henry Clarence Kendall's poem 'Beyond Kerguelen'; though the poets make very different uses of that island, bare of all vegetation, on the whaling route to Antarctic waters.

But these are isolated bits and pieces of an enormous jigsaw whose overall meaning could only be put together out of an encyclopaedic knowledge of various cultural histories. My purpose here is to follow one more limited theme which relates to perceptions of Wales and of Australia, and which starts in the person of T. Harri Jones.

This Anglo-Welsh - or should I say Australian-Welsh? - poet was born into a poor rural family (his father was a foreman roadman) near Llanafan in Powys in 1921. It was an area of marginal upland farms where the Welsh language was in retreat. Unlike his father and grandfather, Harri spoke no Welsh, a characteristic Anglo-Welsh loss which he was later to regret.

In 1939 he come as a student to the English Department at the University College of Wales, Aberystwyth, but the war intervened and from 1941 to 1946 he served in the navy. In 1959 he took up a post teaching English at the Newcastle college of the University of New South Wales. It was in Newcastle, not far from his home, that he was found drowned in a rock-pool in January 1965.

Many Welsh writers of his generation, whether writing in English or Welsh, began their lives in a world of material scarcity and austere

Puritan religion (that was not without its own kind of emotional intensity) but lived to be part of a much more prosperous and broad minded world which nevertheless left them feeling the loss of something important. This tension is seen very clearly in the later work of Kate Roberts, writing in Welsh.

For T. Harri Jones the duality of feeling is enhanced by the move from Wales to Australia. The two countries become symbols of the two lives he has known - one poor, defeated, repressed; the other affluent, relaxed, releasing the senses. A great many of his poems - perhaps the majority, and whether their explicit theme is Wales, or love, derive from the same tension:

> I took for emblem the upland moors and the rocky
> slopes above them, bitter parishes
> Of the buzzard striking from lonely circles
> And the ragged fox hunting the lean
> Rabbits, and the starved preacher nourishing
> A little heat from a hell that once had meaning ...
>
> And now I live in the good meadows, I have
> No emblem except your body, and I am
> Still a member of a narrow chapel, and a boy
> From a hungry parish, a spoiled preacher,
> Greedily taking the surplus of your sunshine,
> And still afraid of hell because I've been there.

('Llanafan Unrevisited') [4]

Those who have been on the fringes of puritan religion perceive it very often entirely in terms of restriction - that is sometimes the case in

Dylan Thomas's stories. But Harri Jones knows too well, from within,

both the repressions and the transposed energies they breed:

> And the capel, God in a little <u>bwthyn</u>
> Once whitewashed - but God in the voices
> Of the mean, the crippled, the green bacon eaters,
> The lead me beside still waters buggers, the wild boys,
> The sin-eaters, and the godly daughters,
> All of them suddenly in unison
> In the ugliest building I have ever seen
> - Pisgah I shall never see again -
> All suddenly bursting - not bursting,
> All suddenly startled into song, to praise
> The God of fornication and the world we live in.
>
> Boyo, if you come from a country like that
> You can talk to me of sin and related matters.
>
> ('The Welshman in Exile Speaks')

In 'Rhiannon' he addresses his seven-year old daughter. She is growing

up in Australia, declares that she too wants to be a poet, and wants to

ride to Ayer's Rock, on a camel from Alice Springs:

> Would the vision of that monolith
> Stay in her mind and dominate her dreams
> As in my mind and dreams of thirty years
> There stays the small hill, Allt-y-clych
> The hill of bells, bedraggled with wet fern
> And stained with sheep, and holding like a threat
> The wild religion and the ancient tongue,
> All the defeated centuries of Wales?

The question is an open one, but the pressure on the Welsh images
compared with her child's picture book perception of Ayer's Rock
suggest the answer 'No'. There might, of course, be another comparison
possible - with the experience of an Aboriginal Australian who had
moved to the city from traditional language and ways.

In Harri Jones's later years, the nationalist challenge was beginning to
surface in Wales, a challenge to those defeated centuries, a challenge to
Welsh people to stay here and do something about the situation. It is
associated with the poetry of R.S. Thomas, much of which addresses
Wales with a bitter loyalty which Harri Jones could well understand. It
is not Dylan Thomas's 'Childhood land' left behind in adult life, but a
botched and defeated land that is still worth the effort of those who will
stay to reclaim it. Harri Jones must have felt the force of R.S. Thomas's
appeal to defend himself so ambivalently:

> BACK?
> (to R.S. Thomas)
>
> Back is the question
> Carried to me on the curlew's wing,
> And the strong sides of the salmon.
>
> Should I go back then
> To the narrow path, the sheep turds,
> And the birded language?
>
> Back to an old, thin bitch
> Fawning on my spit, writhing
> Her lank belly with memories:

Back to the chapel, and the charade
Of the word of God made by a preacher
Without a tongue:

Back to the ingrowing quarrels,
The family where you have to remember
Who is not speaking to whom:

Back to the shamed memories of Glyn Dwr
And Saunders Lewis's aerodrome
And a match at Swansea?

Of course I'd go back if somebody'd pay me
To live in my own country
Like a bloody Englishman.

But for now, lacking the money,
I must be content with the curlew's cry
And the salmon's taut belly

And the waves, of water and of fern
And words, that beat unendingly
On the rocks of the mind's country.

At this point I turn to Harri Webb, a nationalist poet of the Sixties and Seventies much of whose poetry is public and declamatory. He wrote a short poem 'In Memory of Harri Jones' which both sympathises with the emigré and recognizes the impossibility of escape:

You did well to get out of
This hole in the middle of Wales,
Only there is nowhere else
Anywhere.

Another of Harri Webb's poems, 'The Boomerang in the Parlour' [5] posits a second unrealized self for its author. As a young man his father had gone to Australia,

> ....exchanging
> The cramped peninsula for the outback, the frugal
> Patchwork of fields for the prodigal spaces he rode
> Along the rabbit fence or under the soaring jarra.

Returning to Wales after the Gallipoli Campaign, his father brought mementoes of Australia, and nursed the wish that his son would follow in his steps and make the journey there, which Harri Webb never did. But what would have become of him had he gone? The perception in the second half of the poem that every country has to be made new, is I think, an advance on the symbolization of two lands as opposite poles of restriction and opportunity, which may of course be true to a particular individual's experience in a given period, but offers only limited understanding of the countries themselves. For Harri Webb, Wales too remains to be made:

> And so I have
> Another hypothetical Australian self,
> The might-have-been man of a clean new empty country
> Where nearly all the songs have yet to be sung.
> It is this shadow that perhaps has led me
> Past islands of enchantment, capes that could have been
> Called deception, disappointment and farewell,
> To the strange and silent shore where now I stand,
> **Terra Incognita**: a land whose memory
> Has not begun, whose past has been forgotten
> But for a clutter of nightmares and legends and lies.
> This land, too, has a desert at its heart

So far I have dealt with conscious parallels and influences, but for me the comparative study of literature really comes to life not in terms of journeys made from one culture to another, or of perceived borrowings, but when similar themes arise in different societies and testify to something common - not 'universal' nor any such gradiose concept - but something specifically comparable arising from partly similar conditions.

Within Welsh-language literature in recent times one sometimes finds experiences that relate to language itself, experiences that can be parallelled in other minorities where feelings of inferiority, situations of conflict, and the effort to transcend these things, regularly accompany similar linguistic situations. But what of the literature of English-speaking Wales - how is that best understood internationally?

One thing it certainly is not, namely the simple rendering of Welsh-speaking Wales in English. Is it then a regional variant of English literature? Few writers today would accept that, though there was a time when a 'cultural cringe' might have been identified here too, when Welshness was perceived as a kind of local colour required by London publishers.

Or could it be that it is best seen as a 'new literature in English' whose writers are seeking to write in a country named and imagined by another language, who have to define themselves against the powerful metropolitan English and American models, yet by the very fact of writing in English state their distance from the original language and culture of their own place.

Anglo-Welsh literature is strongly concerned, obsessionally even, with relation to place in the sense of <u>landscape</u>. Places are strongly present in Welsh literature too, but more as shared reference, testifying to cultural continuity, to family relationships, to community; rarely does one <u>see</u> the land, however; it is taken for granted.

But any number of Anglo-Welsh poems seek a relationship, through landscape, with the people who have gone before them, and with a language from which they feel banished.   They project their concerns on to the landscape - if only they could merge with it they might truly inherit!

Similar concerns can be found in other places where movement of population or language change have produced cultural disjunction. The West Indian poet and dramatist, Derek Walcott, describes the condition thus: "We have not wholly sunk into our landscape" [6], meaning that the imaginative interpenetration of place and people through language has not yet fully taken place.   At an early stage in his career, Walcott set out to incorporate his island of St. Lucia in the imagination by the simple naming of places and flora and fauna. That was something white Australians had to contend with too.   Voss, in Patrick White's great novel of the same name, accuses them of huddling on the rim of their continent, afraid of the country which for lack of any other they call theirs.   His journey into the interior, indeed the whole book, can be seen as a great imaginative effort at incorporation, through suffering and through identification with the Aboriginal inhabitants.   The heroine of the book, Laura Trevelyan, can write, eventually: "I could now lay my head on the ugliest rock in the land and feel at rest". [7]

I conclude by setting side by side one Australian poem and one Anglo-Welsh, Judith Wright's 'At Cooloolah' [8] and Sam Adam's 'Hill Fort, Caerllion'. [9]   The Australian poem is by far the more self-conscious; in the Anglo-Welsh world it is still a provocation to offer an analysis of our literature as 'colonial', and Anglo-Welsh authors often reveal the symptoms unconsciously.

AT COOLOOLAH

The blue crane fishing in Cooloolah's twilight
has fished there longer than our centuries.
He is the certain heir of lake and evening,
and he will wear their colour till he dies;

but I'm a stranger, come of a conquering people.
I cannot share his calm, who watch his lake,
being unloved by all my eyes delight in
and made uneasy, for an old murder's sake.

Those dark-skinned people who once named Cooloolah
knew that no land is lost or won by wars,
for earth is spirit; the invader's feet will tangle
in nets there and his blood be thinned by fears.

Riding at noon and ninety years ago,
my grandfather was beckoned by a ghost -
a black accoutred warrior armed for fighting,
who sank into bare plain, as now into time past.

White shores of sand, plumed reed and paperbark,
clear heavenly levels frequented by crane and swan -
I know that we are justified only by love,
but oppressed by arrogant guilt, have room for none.

And walking on clean sand among the prints
of bird and animal, I am challenged by a driftwood spear
thrust from the water; and, like my grandfather,
must quiet a heart accused by its own fear.

HILL FORT, CAERLLION

From this tree-finned hill
Breasting the breeze -
Leaf shadows like water shifting,
Sounds of water always moving
In the preening of so many leaves -
I can look down over old Caerllion.

In the aqueous rush of bracken fronds
Breaking round, and in a sound
Clearing now, once heard,
An unbroken hum
Like some instrument endlessly strummed
On one low note, or the tone

Of wires looped from pole
To pole vibrating through wood
Where we pressed our ears,

> There is a sense of something living,
> Breathing, watching here
> As I push towards the rampart mound.
>
> The path is blocked. A swarthy
> Sentry bars the way, this spear -
> Tip sparks with sunlight.
> He challenges in accents I know well;
> The words I recognise but the sense eludes.
> I am ashamed and silent. He runs me through.

Each poem starts with a landscape, but Judith Wright quickly contrasts the calm of the scene, and of the crane who is 'the certain heir' of that scene, with the unease occasioned by the guilt of 'a conquering people' and her own inability to share that calm.   In the third verse and again in the fifth verse there is explicit discussion of how guilt and fear frustrate the unity of person and place.   In the driftwood spear thrust from the water in the final verse, a sharp vertical line against the 'clear heavenly levels' of lake and sand, the landscape recalls her grandfather's real encounter with the black Aboriginal warrior of ninety years ago.

It was the spear, with something of the same sense of archaic menace in each case, that first drew my attention to the comparison.   Sam Adams, too, starts with a landscape which is more gradually and less self-consciously perturbed by the low, vibrating note as the poet approaches the rampart of the old hill-fort.   The poem might at this point seem to be simply about the living presence of the past on a historic site.   What makes it a characteristic Anglo-Welsh poem is still to come: 'He challenges in accents I know well'.   The encounter is

with a past that is different but also familiar, strangely familiar.   It is
with the ancestor on the other side of the language-break.   It produces
shame rather than guilt, a more self-destructive feeling, as the last
phrase makes clear.

No two solutions are the same, and the two poems can easily be used to
show difference as to show similarity.   Yet I hope enough has been
said to show that neither in an 'English' poem, though both are in
English.

Notes

Llanafan Revisited, The Welshman in Exile Speaks, Rhiannon and *Back is the Question* by T. Harri Jones, first appeared in The Collected Poems of T. Harri Jones, published by Gomer Press, Llandysul, and are reporduced here with the permission of the publisher.

Extracts from *In Memory of Harri Jones* and *The Boomerang in the Parlour*, by Harri Webb, are reproduced with the permission of the publisher.

Judith Wright's poem, *At Cooloolah* from Collected Poems, was first published by Collins/Angus & Robertson, North Ryde, NSW, and is reproduced here with the permission of the publisher.

Hill Fort, Caerllion by Sam Adams is reporduced here with the permission of the author.

1.   See Diary of a Welsh Swagman 1869-94 ed. William Evans. Melbourne: Macmillan 1975. Also 'The Swagman from Trecefel' in Planet 61, 1987.

2.   'A Tribute to Old Delight' in Planet 66, 1987.

3.   In Dail Pren, Gwasg Aberystwyth, 1967.

4.   Quotations are from The Collected Poems of T. Harri Jones, edited and with an introduction by Julian Croft and Don Dale-Jones. Llandysul: Gomer Press 1977. Julian Croft is also the author of T.H. Jones in the Writers of Wales series, Cardiff, University of Wales Press 1976.

5.   Both poems are to be found in The Green Desert by Harri Webb, Gomer, Llandysul 1969.

6.   In 'What the Twilight Says: An Overture' printed as preface to
       the volume of Walcott plays <u>Dream on Monkey Mountain and
       Other Plays</u>, New York: Farrar, Strauss 1970.

7.   <u>Voss</u>, Penguin edition p. 239.

8.   In <u>Five Senses</u>, Sydney: Angus and Robertson 1963.

9.   In <u>Poems '73</u> Llandysul: Gomer 1973.

Coal-Mining Communities: The Welsh And Australian Experience Compared

Gareth Rees

Introduction

In the spring of 1988, there was substantial newspaper coverage which described a new deal with a Japanese company, Showa Shell Sekiyu, designed to expand the export of Rhondda coal to Japan above its existing level of 200,000 tonnes per annum. Now, for those who recall those other newspaper reports which mourned the demise of the last pit in the Rhondda in 1986, this may seem rather puzzling. However, if it is added that the report was carried by the *Australian Financial Review* (15 March 1988) and that the Rhondda referred to is a colliery complex just outside Ipswich in southern Queensland, the paradox is resolved.

The point of the anecdote, of course, is to emphasise the theme of this chapter: the continuities and contrasts between the experience of the coal industry and coal-mining in Wales and Australia. At an immediate level, the continuities are striking. The Rhondda complex referred to earlier is located in the township of Ebbw Vale. In New South Wales, it is possible to visit the suburbs of Swansea and Cardiff in the great coal and steel port of Newcastle; in the now largely derelict South Maitland coalfield in the Lower Hunter Valley, one can see the villages of Neath and Aberdare and the sites of long-closed collieries such as Stanford Merthyr.

Underpinning these shared place-names, of course, there is a long history of human migration from Wales to work in the Australian coalfields. For the Welsh visitor it is rather moving to discover in the cemetry of the town of Kurri Kurri, again in the heart of the South Maitland field, tucked away in the sections reserved for the Baptists and the Congregationalists, head-stone after head-stone, many with Welsh inscriptions, dedicated to the memories of Welsh Australians killed in accidents at the nearby Stanford Merthyr colliery (which is where most of the Welsh emigrants worked, at least initially). More directly, there are still individual life-histories which encapsulate the human links between the coal-mining areas of the two countries. For example, Evan Phillips, who was National President of the Miners' Federation (the Australian equivalent of the NUM) during the 1970s, emigrated from the (Welsh) Rhondda with his Communist, coal-mining parents to Cessnock (again in the South Maitland field) in 1922 and he subsequently pursued his career as an Australian miner and industrial and political activist; a 'Welsh' career which was exceptional only by reason of his eventual election to senior office within his trade union.

At a more systematic level, too, there is a sense of shared experience between the coal-mining communities of Wales and Australia. When a respondent, a lodge official from Collinsville, a 'Little Moscow' in the far north of Queensland, explained the international comradeship of coal-miners in terms of their common experiences, he was in effect articulating a powerful strand within social and political theory. More so than for any other occupational group, the social experience of coal-miners has been described in simple, one-dimensional terms (solidarity; industrial and political militancy; cultural conservatism, sexual chauvinism; etc.) and has been 'explained' in terms of the structural imperatives of working conditions in the mines and of living conditions in coalfield communities. [2]   In view of the actual historical linkages, it is not surprising that this commonality of social experience should be particularly powerfully conceived in both Wales and Australia.

Imagined Communities

One manifestation of this is in the political sphere. In both countries, there is a deep well of social imagery about miners, drawn upon equally by the political Left and Right. For the Right, the 'folk memory' is of the threat posed by the miners to conservative governments and even, more widely, to the very stability of society itself. For the Left, of course, exactly the same historical record determines that the miners are the 'shock troops' of the labour movement. Royden Harrison, writing of the 1974 national miners' strike in Britain, describes the collective perspective very vividly:

> It was ordained that the coal miners as the archetypal proletarians and folk heroes of their class were going to conquer: were going to reduce the editors of *The Times* and *The Economist* to the most fearful incoherence: were going to lead a petulant Prime Minister, wilfully ignorant of the lessons of Labour History, to his political destruction. [3]

Or, as another eminent historian, Raphael Samuel, this time writing about the 1984-1985 stike in Britain, puts it:

> In one aspect the strike was a war of ghosts, in which the living actors were dwarfed by the shadows they had conjured up. [4]

Significantly, this popular political imagery is paralleled by and even feeds upon, a theoretical imagery constructed in the work of historians and sociologists of the miners. This is clearly not the place to rehearse this particular conventional wisdom in detail. However, it is important to sketch its essential features. In this task, the work of Martin Bulmer [5] is a convenient resource. What Bulmer does is to present what he describes, after Max Weber, as an 'ideal type' of the mining community, which embodies a set of essential structural characteristics. These, in turn, provide the necessary context for the development of what is seen as the distinctive industrial and political militancy and combativeness of the miners.

In these terms, then, the 'mining community' is geographically isolated from other industrial activities, as a result of the straightforward geology and technology of mining. The latter, in turn, generates a highly distinctive set of working conditions, in which miners share common experiences of unpleasant and highly dangerous work. Moreover, these working conditions also imply high levels of occupational homogeneity amongst miners, with a relative absence of hierarchy. Miners enjoy characteristically communal forms of leisure activity, in which work-place relationships are reinforced. Whilst within the family, gender roles are highly segregated, with women almost singly-handedly responsible for domestic work, 'servicing' their men and enabling the latter's participation in mining work. In these ways, the characteristic features of both production and community life combine to constitute the structural basis for highly solidary forms of social relations, which are expressed in the peculiarly militant and peculiarly 'macho' industrial and political cultures of the coalfields.

Now, in spite of the strength of this kind of conceptualisation in both Wales and Australia, it is suggested here that it is an ill-founded analysis. As one Australian sociologist, Andrew Metcalfe, puts it:

> The tradition of the quintessential proletarian coal-miner is a subtle insult to the history of miners. It neglects the differentiation among miners and the variety of their political responses to class structures. It neglects the partial nature of these responses, and the ambivalence of their relation with the bourgeois challengers. Once the heroic model of class strugle is enshrined on a museum pedestal, class struggle can no longer be recognised in the shabbier guises it wears among coalminers in everyday life. [6]

In his study of the social relations of the South Maitland coalfield during the early/middle decades of the present century, Metcalfe draws a distinction between what he sees as **two** characteristic modes of response by miners to the exploitations of the coal-owners: on the one hand, the 'respectable' tradition, embodying the ethics of self-discipline, collective action and, ultimately, a socialist political project; on the other, the 'larrikin' mode of response, embodying

> the constellation of ... traits which include mateship, beer drinking, gambling, swearing, joking, fighting, vulgarity, virility and physical prowess. The larrikin is masculine, self-assertive and self-reliant when left to his own resources. [7]

The latter response, despite its dramatic rejection of 'desirable', bourgeois mores, is, of course, a defensive one, concerned with preserving the limited social space available in customary work practices and the sub-culture of the coal towns. It is a response associated with the absenteeism and numerous petty stoppages immortalised in the song about going 'on strike because the sun did shine' (a temptation much stronger in Australia than Wales!)

Metcalfe associates the 'respectable' tradition with the miners' leadership and describes their attempt to discipline the 'larrikinism' of the rank-and-file. It is doubtful, however, whether this kind of neat attribution of responses is especially useful. Certainly, it seems to me that there is ample evidence in the Welsh situation which suggests a more complex intermingling of the two responses. For example, nobody could deny the seriousness of purpose or the political sophistication of those many Welsh miners who were active in the organisation of the 1984-1985 strike ('respectable' activity, in Metcalfe's terms). At the same time, much of the genuine enjoyment of the strike for many of these same activists derived from the freedom which they had to express precisely those traits associated with 'larrikinism'; and the conservative, defensive character of the strike has been frequently remarked upon. [8] What is important to retain from Metcalfe's discussion, however, is his recognition of the complexity of the social experience of mining and the reductionism implied in any attempt to 'read off' the supposed character of that experience from the structural characteristics of mining or mining communities. Again, as he says:

> The larrikin and respectable consciousnesses were not formulated as coherent philosophies, but as responses to certain challenges which the miners faced in their lives ...; the difference between the larrikin and respectable perspectives did not reflect different steps up the ladder to 'raised class consciousness', but the irresolvability of different problems faced in working class practice. [9]

An alternative perspective on the shortcomings of the conventional conceptualisation of miners is provided by an examination of the distinctiveness of the different areas in the Australian coalfield. Again, it is possible only to touch upon some of the complexities involved here. Many of the miners and union officials who participated in the study were careful to explain the differences between New South Wales mining and that in Queensland. New South Wales is the historical focus of the Australian industry, developing from the earliest days of the convict settlements, and generating powerful - if complex, as has been suggested - traditions around its underground mines. Production remains predominantly from underground working, despite the growth of open-cut mining from the mid 1970s. [10] Queensland too has a long history of underground mining in its West Moreton field around Ipswich in the far south of the state. [11] However, production here was always on quite a small scale and it was not until the development of the massive open-cut mines in central Queensland from the late 1960s onwards that Queensland came to play a significant role in the Australian and, indeed, international coal industry. By the end of the 1980s Queensland produced almost the same amount of coal as New South Wales, but almost all of it by open-cut methods (althought this may, of course, change in the future).

Quite simply, coal-miners in Queensland conform only in very partial ways with the characteristics conventionally associated with their occupational group. [12] For the most part, they were recruited 'green' to mining from the surrounding rural areas. Their politics were generally conservative, the majority voting for the National Party. The mining to which they were introduced bears a closer resemblance to large-scale construction work than to deep-mining (indeed, in Britain, open-cast mining is organised by the Transport and General Workers' Union, rather than the National Union of Mineworkers - although it is possible that the latter are now regretting this). Even the towns which were built to house the miners and their families, whilst isolated and 'single-industry' in the manner of traditional coal towns, bore none of the meanness and poverty associated with the latter and indeed, were more mixed in their class composition, as professional, technical and supervisory staff were also obliged to live there.

What is, perhaps, most intriguing here is that, despite these unconventional structural characteristics, it is often claimed that the Queensland miners have taken on much of the industrial militancy associated with their underground comrades. [13] In part, it is argued,

this is the result of the insensitivity of the management strategy
implemented by the American multi-national mining company,
the Utah Development Company, which played the dominant role in
the central Queensland developments (until a buy-out in 1983 by the
Australian multi-national, Broken Hill Proprietary). Equally, the
major mining union, the Miners' Federation, devoted considerable
resources to creating a stable organisational structure in the new mines,
which both 'educated' the 'green' workers and provided the basis for
collective action. [14] Nevertheless, it is instructive that Andrew
Vickers, the President of the Queensland Colliery Employees' Union
(the Queensland District of the Miners' Federation) conceded to me that
the militancy of his membership was highly economistic - 'you can get
them out when their hip pockets are affected' - and largely divorced
from any wider political project. Indeed, many of the Queensland
miners remain loyal to the National Party (which, incidentally, through
the rather eccentric state government of Sir Joh Bielke Petersen, was
for many years busy enacting stiff anti-union legislation).

Even in New South Wales, where - as has been shown - the structural
characteristics of the mining communities was more conventional,
there are parallels with this complexity of political response. Again,
Metcalfe's account is revealing; he says

> The case of pit-top meetings indicates that the miners'
> practice did not simply follow the application of a
> coherent and shared political consciousness. Political
> consensuses were continually being constructed and

shifted in the course of political struggle between miners.
Speakers at the pit-top strove to mobilise their colleagues
behind different constellations of ideas, in response to
different situations. Thus the same miners who
collectively defied their leaders during sunshine strikes
might be collectively loyal to their Australian Labor Party
representatives in parliamentary elections, but vote for
Communists in Miners' Federation Ballots. Miners could
call on a wide range of ideas and beliefs that could be
assembled to form an even wider range of political
perspectives. [15]

Similarly, whilst the results of the 1988 state elections in New South
Wales, in which there were massive swings against the Australian
Labor Party in the coal and steel heartlands of the Hunter Valley and
the Illawarra, are in part attributable to the declining significance of
traditional occupations in those regions, they also serve as a salutory
reminder (to the Australia Labor Party, as well as social commentators)
that it is quite simply foolhardy to attempt to reduce the complexity of
the social experience of mining communities to simplistic theoretical
formulae.

The recent history of coal-mining in Britain also provides ample
evidence of the limitations of the conventional characterisation.
During the 1984-1985 miners' strike, Arthur Scargill, the national
President of the National Union of Mineworkers, was fond of finishing
his speeches with the cry 'The miners united will never be defeated!'.
Whatever the reaction of the activists who flocked to hear him, the
simple reality was that the miners were **not** united: strike action had
never been taken by the overwhelming majority of miners in the

Nottingham and other Midlands coalfields, whilst support in other areas - including some of the ones with 'militant' traditions - faded dramatically from the autumn of 1984 onwards. Whilst in part this diversity of political response may be accounted for in terms of the real differences in material conditions - both within the industry and more generally - betwen the various parts of the British coalfields, it also reflects a genuine complexity of social experience and construction of political activity . [16]

Even those areas which were especially active in the prosecution of the strike cannot be reduced to straightforward homogeneity. As Samuel has remarked,

> Arthur Scargill was viewed with some suspicion in the Welsh and Scottish coalfields, which had their own local heroes and their own distinctive version of militancy - more 'educated', more Communist, more statesmanlike than those characteristic of the Barnsley and Doncaster coalfields. [17]

These alternative constructions of a left position within the British coalfield have, if anything, become even more acute in the aftermath of the defeat of the strike. In the face of a concerted drive by the industry's management to force through radical changes, the kinds of tensions and inconsistencies to which Metcalfe refers in the Australian context, have become only too apparent. In South Wales, for example, whatever the views of what remains of the 'rank-and-file', it is clear that the NUM's Area leadership has become increasingly hostile to the 'militant' strategy being pursued by the national President, Arthur Scargill.

What should be stressed, then, is the element of **contingency** which shapes the social experience of coal-miners (as much as anyone else). Whilst it is, of course, true that structural conditions set constraints on that experience, it is important not to lose sight of the power of human agency in creating the culture through which political and industrial reponses are constructed.

> People face social relations which exist beyond their individual control; in making history they must respond to challenges posed by these structures; their responses will be constrained by the structures. This does not, however, imply that the history-making responses can be straightforwardly 'read off' the class structure, for there are mediating realms wherein the connections between class structures and observable class struggle become tangled or even torn". [18]

Challenging Coal Restructuring

This kind of analysis of coalfield experience also contributes to the understanding of the changes which have taken place in the industries of the two countries during the 1980s. Both industries have experienced very rapid changes in the technology of coal extraction and associated patterns of work organisation; these in turn have resulted in colliery closures and job losses. In both countries, there have been major industrial conflicts over the terms on which these changes are introduced. Nevertheless, there are fundamental differences between what has happened in Australia and what has happened in Wales, and Britain more widely.

In Australia, the coal companies have attempted to raise levels of labour productivity and the intensity of capital utilisation through the improvement of open-cut technology (larger machines, capable of operating with deeper over-burdens and so forth) and through the introduction of the most advanced long-wall mining techniques in their deep-mines in both Queensland and New South Wales. These changes, in turn, required the development of 365-day per year coaling (the abandonment of the 'Australian Weekend' in the coal industry) and consequent changes in shift patterns and other work practices. The achievement of such a programme has facilitated the closure of mines which became 'unprofitable' and the more general loss of job opportunities (although the employers dispute this).

In Wales, as part of the more general restructuring of the British coal industry in the aftermath of the 1984-1985 strike, there has been a massive reduction in employment and the closure of many collieries. However, given that this has been paralleled by the introduction of new, heavy-duty face technology in most of the remaining pits and the growth of open-cast mining, actual output has remained more or less constant, with the result that productivity figures have soared and the coalfield was even on occasion hovering on the brink of profitability for the first time in many decades.

However, the market conditions experienced by the two coal industries are fundamentally different. The Australian industry is massively orientated towards exporting into the industrial economies of South East Asia (and, in particular, Japan) and of Europe. The companies were forced into restructuring (in what is already one of the most efficient coal industries in the world) by the long-term price pressures imposed by the massive over-supply of both coking and steaming coal on the world market. The British industry, on the other hand, whatever the history of areas such as South Wales, now exports virtually nothing and is tied to the domestic supply of the Central Electricity Generating Board and the British Steel Corporation. Accordingly, the pressures upon British Coal to increase productivity have derived from the political priorities of the current government. What this means, then, is that the bargaining space available to miners and their organisations in the two countries has been vastly different, as a result of these differing structual conditions. Whereas the Australian miners had something to bargain with, it is very difficult to see what could be salvaged in the British and Welsh situation, given the government's apparent willingness to substitute imported for domestically produced coal; a trend which has undoubtedly been intensified with the privatisation of electricity generation and steel-making.

Over and above this, however, the responses of miners to the conditions which face them are very different in the two countries. The National Union of Miners has been torn apart in the period since the miners' strike by conflicts over whether outright opposition to restructuring or an attempt to ameliorate the terms on which it takes place is the most effective strategy in current circumstances. The mining unions in Australia, on the other hand, have not only remained united (althought this unity may be tested by further closures and job losses) but have stuck firm to a strategy which involves the negotiation (occasionally backed up by limited strike action) of the best terms for the implementation of new technology and practices. Clearly, there is nothing inevitable about these contrasting outcomes in the two industries; it is precisely here that elements of contingency and human agency are most influential.

It is perhaps the supreme irony that it is this element of human agency which may ultimately determine that just as the only Rhondda exporting coal to Japan is from Australia, so the only Welsh coal may well be from **New** rather than **Old** South Wales.

Notes

1. This chapter derives from research carried out in 1988, involving interviews with - *inter alia* - representatives of the coal companies in Australia and leaders - past and present - of the miners' unions. The research was made possible by a grant from the Nuffield Foundation, whose support is gratefully acknowledged.

2. This argument is discussed more fully in Gareth Rees, 'Class, Community and the Miners', <u>Sociology</u>, 25, forthcoming.

3. Royden Harrison (ed.), <u>The Independent Collier</u>, Brighton, Harvester, 1978, p.2.

4. Raphael Samuel, 'Introduction' in Raphael Samuel, Barbara Bloomfield and Guy Boanas (eds.), <u>The Enemy Within: pit villages and the miners' strike of 1984-85</u>, London; Routledge, 1986, p.6.

5. Martin Bulmer, 'Sociological Models of the Mining Community', <u>Sociological Review</u>, NS23, 1975, 61-92.

6. Andrew Metcalfe, For Freedom and Dignity, Phd thesis, Department of Anthropology, University of Sydney, 1986. (Subsequently published as <u>For Freedom and Dignity: historical agency and class structures in the coalfields of NSW</u>, Sydney; Allen and Unwin, 1988, p.192).

7. <u>For Freedom and Dignity: historical agency and class structures in the coalfields of NSW</u>, op.cit., p.190.

8. For example, Hywel Francis and Gareth Rees, '"No surrender in the Valleys": the 1984-85 miners' strike in south Wales', <u>Llafur: the Journal of Welsh Labour History</u>, 5, 1989, 41-71.

9. <u>For Freedom and Dignity: historical agency and class structures in the coalfields of NSW</u>, op.cit., p.201.

10.   Katherine Gibson, 'Industrial Reorganisation and Coal Production in Australia, 1986-1982: an historical materialist analysis', <u>Australian Geographical Studies,</u> 22, 1984, 221-242.

11.   Pete Thomas, <u>The Coalminers of Queensland: Volume 1 Creating the Traditions</u>, Ipswich: Queensland Colliery Employees Union, 1986.

12.   Claire Williams, <u>Open Cut: the working class in an Australian mining town</u>, Sydney: George Allen and Unwin, 1981.

13.   For example, Pete Thomas, <u>Miners in the 1970s,</u> Sydney: Miners' Federation, 1983.

14.   Interview with Evan Philips, former President of the Miners' Federation.

15.   <u>For Freedom and Dignity: historical agency and class structures in the coalfields of NSW</u>, op.cit., p.198.

16.   Gareth Rees, 'Regional restructuring, class change and political action: preliminary comments on the 1984-85 miners' strike in South Wales', <u>Society and Space,</u> 3, 1985, 389-406.

17.   <u>The Enemy Within: pit villages and the miners' strike of 1984-85,</u> op.cit., p.19.

18.   <u>For Freedom and Dignity: historical agency and class structures in the coalfields of NSW</u>, op.cit.

MINORITIES IN A BROADCAST CULTURE: THE WELSH AND AUSTRALIAN EXPERIENCE

J.G. Menham

Cultural Connections and Parallels between Wales and Australia have a particular significance in an exploration of indigenous broadcasting and its contribution to the wider issue of minority programming. [1] The connecting link is, of course, language, and among the parallels of the cultural experience are the almost spiritual significance of the landscape, the vibrant depth of indigenous culture, and its self conscious reassertion against external threat.

Most people's views of their social surroundings, the national and international world, their intellectual thinking, their attitudes and behaviour have at some time been and are continuing to be affected by their association with television.   Television thus has subtle but profound effects on our perception of the world, the particular society in which we live and on our national character.

The general disposition of the entertainment media, in this sociological context, to cater for a mass audience has served to focus attention on a new national responsibility: minority programming.

In the hands of programme makers with what might be called a minority vision, broadcasting has the potential to create a new dimension of understanding, quality and ideas both within and between societies and nations. To do so, however, requires the development of special structures. Governments have a part to play in underpinning these structures, to the extent that they fund public service broadcasting which has a special responsibility beyond that of commercial broadcasting. The perception of commercial broadcasters as having little interest in programmes that meet the specialised needs of small segments of the audience further serves to enhance and define the role of broadcasting institutions funded from the public purse, particularly in so far as they serve the interests of national and indigenous minorities. This has been the special case of the Welsh television channel, S4C. Australia, in turn, has offered its own solutions to indigenous broadcasting, but with definite parallels, not always readily understood, to the Welsh experience.

As in the United Kingdom, the Australian broadcasting system draws a fundamental legal distinction between licensed commercial broadcasting on the one hand and, on the other, national (or public service) broadcasting, which consists in Australia of the Australian Broadcasting

Corporation and the Special Broadcasting Service, the latter with an emphasis on multiculturalism. Indigenous people have long recognised that one of the instruments of cultural preservation is the media, and one of the significant developments in Australia in the last decade has been the way indigenous people have become involved in broadcasting. For the most part it is they who have driven the debate on the relationship between culture and broadcasting. They have been the innovators.

In 1984 the Australian Government, responding to this initiative, established the *Task Force on Aboriginal Broadcasting and Communications.* The report of the task force, <u>Out of the Silent Land</u> [2], has become a landmark document, accepted in its entirety as Australian Government policy. While the Task Force learnt much from an examination of the indigenous situation in Canada, which has led the field in satellite communications to remote areas, it attempted to construct an approach that was essentially Australian. As a consequence of the Task Force Report and its acceptance by Government, the objectives of Aboriginal broadcasting policies in Australia are:

> (i) to develop and extend Australian broadcasting and telecommuniciations in order to reinforce and promote the cultural identity of Aboriginals,
>
> (ii) to ensure that Aboriginals are given the opportunity to participate in radio and television broadcasting and communications,

(iii) to create wider appreciation of Aboriginal culture and identity.

The strategy developed by the Task Force was based on:

(i) the coordinated introduction of satellite radio and television reception and rebroadcasting facilities to remote Aboriginal communities,

(ii) the provision of facilities to allow Aboriginals to control programmes broadcast to their communities,

(iii) the extension of existing radio services including the High Frequency Inland radio service,

(iv) the encouragement of Aboriginal participation in radio and television production,

(v) the development of Aboriginal broadcasting initiatives by the ABC, commercial broadcasters and the public broadcasting sector.

Australia's geographic vastness and sparseness have presented problems not encountered in the more compact Welsh society.   As a consequence, the strategy of broadcasting for the indigenous population in the remote areas in which they live is based not on a single national station but on a network of regional resource broadcasting groups and the installation of 70 Aboriginal community radio and television stations fed by satellite.   These stations give communities control of their broadcasting including the capacity to make local programmes in their own language.

A significant development in remote-area broadcasting services during 1986-87 was the decision by the Australian Broadcasting Tribunal to award the central zone commercial satellite television licence to Imparja, an Aboriginal company established by the Central Australian Aboriginal Media Association (CAAMA). This service now provides both general television programmes and specialised indigenous programmes to viewers in remote areas of the Northern Territory and South Australia where a significant proportion of the audience is Aboriginal. Financial difficulties have plagued the service, denying it the opportunity to become what it would truly wish to become: the equivalent of S4C in Wales.

One of the overriding considerations in the development of Aboriginal broadcasting in Australia has been the concept of 'embedding', enunciated by the Task Force on Aboriginal Broadcasting; a concept which has also had the effect of placing indigenous broadcasting into a wider national context. To quote from the Task Force Report:

> Embedding relates to the nature of communication. One-way broadcasting is in itself a language, a process by which something is communicated to someone. It provides a framework for the way events are assessed. That language should be distinctive to each country. In Australia it should reflect the Australian condition. Embedded within the language typifying a particular country are certain components reflecting special aspects of the land. If this language is to be distinctively Australian, it should relate uniquely to Aboriginal Australia.

It is this concept of embedding which provides the important link between indigenous broadcasting and minority programming, both of which have been successfully combined in the Channel 4 experience in Britain.

In one way or another, we are all a member of some minority and thus share similar concerns about culture, identity, access and opportunity. The threatened indigenous minorities seem more able to express the worth of these things.   In this sense, therefore, traditional minorities inform the situation of national minorities.

Comparing their experience, it is possible to speak of a new minority movement in broadcasting, and to identify opportunities for bringing them together and linking them in an international network, to serve and articulate their interests, and to make a virtue of their difference. Through the use of Aboriginal native languages, broadcasting is providing the foundation for sustaining and promoting Aboriginal culture.

In recent years, various approaches to minority programming have been stimulated by new philosophies of pluralism and multiculturalism, which have set minority broadcasting within a wider social context. Minority broadcasting, in turn, has become something of a benchmark of performance for broadcasting institutions, setting examples in style, form, innovation, quality and excellence.   The source of this inspiration has come from two main directions; first, a liberating view of audience and programming, associated with a recognition of minority interests, and, second, a reinvigoration of the creative spirit stimulated, in the case of the United Kingdom, by a legislative remit to be innovative, while at the same time serving interests other than those catered for by the general services.   This latter approach has been associated with a much broader movement of broadcasting reform, characterised by pressure to widen the sources of programming, to provide for access broadcasting and to introduce more pluralism in ideas, attitudes and voices.

One outcome has been a recognition and reinforcement of the impact of broadcasting on that complex web we call national culture.   As well as a vehicle of entertainment, broadcasting is being seen as a social and cultural tool, widening discourse, admitting new voices, and stimulating literature and the arts.   Taken together, these developments suggest that while imaginative programming is ultimately in the hands of professionals, the Government can provide an environment in which the creative spirit can develop, if not flourish.   This has been the experience of Channel 4 in Britain, with S4C in Wales.

The essential feature of Channel 4 has been the way it has built a schedule around a commitment to minorities and a legislative requirement to be innovative.   From its inception, Channel 4 has become the touchstone against which all programming is coming to be judged.   While the specific structure of Channel 4 may not be exportable (it is linked in a complex way to advertising revenue from commercial television franchise holders), its underlying philosophy can be, both in terms of its financial independence, its publishing model, the way it draws its programming from independent producers and its legislatively prescribed commitment to innovation.   What have been the identifiable signposts of the new creativity associated with the Channel 4 model?

1.   A new creative approach to broadcasting has broadened the base of programming, opening it up to new ideas, and widening programme horizons.

2.   There has been a new commitment to culture.

3.   Independent production groups have established a new industry.

4.   Innovation and creativity have produced a quest for new forms.

5.   The serving of minority interests has led to a widening of choice.

6.   Public service broadcasting ideals are being restored, and re-stated.

7.   New audiences have led to new understanding among groups within society of each other.

8.   There has been a sensitive presentation of language.

9.   New ideas have been developed in co-production and in art forms.

10.   The film industry has been reinvigorated.

11.   Programmes are demonstrating a greater relevance to the viewers' life and culture.

12.   A much wider spectrum of programming has provided both a more comprehensive and a more specialised view of contemporary life.

While some might question the mass appeal of the product, it is nevertheless reinvigorating the form, content and appeal of broadcasting at a time when it is in need of some resuscitation and when public service broadcasting in particular is under close scrutiny, if not external threat.

Such television scheduling is new in the sense of how minorities are being acknowledged as comprising parts of what we have come to think of as the mass audience; new in the sense of how they are being discovered and represented; new in the sense of how they are breaking up the broadcasting schedules into definable and manageable sectors; new in the sense of the imagination and originality they are inspiring; new in the increased understanding of minorities as part of the social fabric; and new in the way ethno-cultural minorities are validating and reinforcing their own identity while speaking to the nation.

Access of minority cultures and viewpoints to the media can re-define an understanding of multiculturalism as an expression of the worth and value of individual identity. Multiculturalism has come to mean different things to different people. In Australia it has tended to be interpreted through the narrow focus of ethnicity rather than as a comprehension of community and cultural diversity in its broadest sense and in all its forms. This view of multiculturalism as ethnicity tends to isolate essential elements of multiculturalism at the margin, divorcing them from mainstream movements and aggregation, and thus depriving them of some of their inherent strength and vitality. This is significant in the Australian broadcasting situation where a distinction has been drawn between the role of the ABC (in terms of national identity), on the one hand, and the SBS (multiculturalism), on the other. It is difficult to see how the two can be separated, or what distinguishes them, unless it is merely a question of degree rather than kind.

The contribution of indigenous and ethnic cultures is an essential element of multiculturalism. These cultures add another dimension to our cultural life and experience, recognising that while we belong to one nation we share a diversity of historical and cultural backgrounds. In this way, multiculturalism draws its patterns from a uniqueness of personal history and experience as well as association. Cultural affinity is particularly important in a multicultural society because, among other things, it enriches that society, demonstrating that culture is not static but a living thing, influenced by a range of social processes, manifesting itself over a wide range of activities and most evident in specific cultural activities, such as the performing arts and broadcasting.

Society is thus built on a wide spectrum of "minority" interests, some of them more fundamental, more enduring and more complex than others.   Minority audiences can exist on their own or can be constructed around a coalition of these interests.   Giving expression to them widens the national discourse and enriches the national culture. Society needs all the articulated experience and viewpoints it can get. The Welsh-born historian, Professor Raymond Williams, told a seminar before his recent death,

> The extreme complexity of any historical and social process being lived out in a particular place at a particular time, the extreme complexity of the interaction of individual lives with all these general conditions, means that you can never at any time think that you have enough voices or that you have representative voices, or that anybody can say in advance what are the important things either to be said or to be written about.

This need for many voices Professor Williams saw as a condition of the cultural health of any complex society.   It lies at the heart of multiculturalism.   Inherent in multiculturalism is freedom of thought, expression and cultural affinity.   There is both a social need and a social responsibility in support for it. Multiculturalism is equity and access in a more public sense, inherent in which are our rights as individuals and the way we interact with the society around us, not only being inspired by it but helping in turn to re-shape it.   The role of broadcasting in a multicultural society is to provide the opportunity and access for this cultural expression — for that is what it is — to admit all the voices of a society.   The important consideration so far as broadcasting is concerned is to regularise the scheduling of multicultural programming so as not to separate it out as a multicultural activity in the perception of the audience, but for it to be seen as a part of general programming, reflecting society's diversity.   In this way it becomes a normal and accepted part of viewing and of life, a deliberate and regular exposure which is made possible through national broadcasters not committed to the ratings.   The problem of the relatively isolated minority is overcome, and perhaps, in time, it no longer becomes necessary to speak of multiculturalism as a policy objective but to observe its practical application through cultural growth.

The distinctive element in Channel 4's approach to multiculturalism is, in the words of Farrukh Dhondy, Channel 4's commissioning editor for multicultural programmes, that "we re-discovered monocultural programming of different monocultures and called it multicultural". It was to be diverse, but moreover it was to be continuous.   In terms of practical outcomes this has meant Asian and Black current affairs programmes at peak time, distinct Black and Asian comedy series, Black feature films, a Black drama series, 40 Black and Third World documentary programmes a year, regular Hindi film seasons, two Black music shows, serialised Pakistani drama and an Asian chat show, all of which adds up to something of a revolution in national scheduling.

This revolution has meant the continuing presence of ethno-cultural minorities in Channel 4's programming and thus in the national consciousness. While it may not necessarily be changing attitudes, it is creating awareness of these groups and through that awareness greater understanding of their situation. It is also making for better television. Above all it underlines the responsibility of national public broadcasting authorities and the capacity of Government to provide the necessary framework for such programming. The Welsh television arrangements reinforce this approach, the Fourth Television Channel in Wales being created under the *Broadcasting Act 1981:*

(i)   to provide television programmes (other than advertisements) of high quality for broadcasting by the IBA on the Fourth Channel in Wales, and

(ii)   to provide the IBA with programme schedules for those programmes.

The Act provides that a substantial proportion of the programmes included in the programme schedules provided by the Welsh Authority shall be in Welsh, and especially between 6.30 p.m. and 10.00 p.m. In this respect, the fourth channel in Wales is proclaimed as a public service for disseminating information, education and entertainment.

There is inevitably a mixed reaction to the cost of providing the service, now 20 per cent of ITV advertising funds devoted to Channel 4 (an estimated £45 million).   Some argue that this is an unnecessary extravagance.   Others, however, argue that it has been responsible for maintaining a cultural autonomy and identity within the dominant British culture.   It is part of a movement of bringing the languages of new groups to the screen, conveying life experiences across boundaries of language and country.

Considered by some to be a quaint expression of a strange language, regarded by others as the ultimate protection of the Welsh nation, S4C is the exclamation mark of minority broadcasting, underscoring what a commitment to minority broadcasting in its broadest sense, and to indigenous broadcasting in its narrowest sense, can do.

It is not insignificant that S4C's account of its first five years of operation was called *Television Wales — A New Industry.* [3] Apart from reinvigorating Welsh culture, it has created a new wave of independent production, has pioneered the development of feature films in Welsh, and has won awards for both its film production and animation.   Pervading the whole Welsh television scene is an excitement and creativity which can be attributed directly to S4C, reflecting on a regional scale what Channel 4 has done to British television generally.

The impact of broadcasting on multiculturalism as a microcosm of Australian society will flow, as it has done in Britain, from the embedding of a range of quality and experimental programmes in the national broadcasting schedules. More importantly the structure of the industry is such that this embedding will come from the public service broadcasting system rather than commercial broadcasting.

S4C in Wales offers a specific example of the path Australian television could follow in the future development of the Special Broadcasting Service. There, a basic distinction — as with the national Channel 4 — has been drawn between the transmission of the service and the commissioning of programmes. The result has been a new spirit of innovation and creativity, and the creation of a new industry based on independent production. S4C more than any other institution (albeit in a specific regional context) demonstrates how the commitment to minorities combined with an appropriate independent structure and statutory base has reinvigorated the broadcasting schedules.

It is within the capacity of Government, in developing the fundamental relationship between it and national broadcasters, to create an environment which supports creative and innovative approaches to programming — the essential core of broadcasting performance. Moreover, the British experience suggests that the various elements cannot be divorced from each other. Embedding within national programme schedules remains the appropriate way of communicating the ideals of a multicultural society.

The wave of reform which has continued in Britain has had its impact on other national broadcasters.   In the midst of it, Channel 4 and its specific S4C cousin, remain as symbols of how future television might be organised.   But such is the nature of the proposed reforms in Britain, that Channel 4 will continue to have to justify itself.

Countries like Australia will continue to look to Channel 4 for lessons. These lessons are valuable, provided it is realised that Channel 4 was developed for a particular purpose at a particular time in Britain and under particular circumstances.   If, however, one sees in it an expansion of audience commitment, quality and innovative programming, meeting tastes not generally catered for with financial independence to enable it to implement its charter, then Channel 4 remains a model worthy of emulation. Its Welsh cousin underscores a commitment to indigenous broadcasting in its purest sense.   While it continues to broadcast, the Welsh language will remain alive and with it a distinctive Welsh culture.   Such also is the aim of indigenous broadcasting in Australia.

Notes

1.   In preparing for publication the papers presented at the "Wales and Australia" seminar in 1988, the Editors asked me if I could expand my original paper to cover some of the ground I traversed in my study of multicultural broadcasting as a Visiting Fellow at Cambridge. In view of some significant developments in indigenous broadcasting in Australia since the *Wales and Australia* seminar, the advancement in my own thinking as a result of the Fellowship, and the similarities between Welsh broadcasting and indigenous broadcasting in Australia, I readily took the opportunity to expand the paper which now appears in this form for the first time.

2.   <u>Out of the Silent Land; Report of the Task Force on Aboriginal Broadcasting and Communications</u>: Canberra, Australian Government Publishing Service, 1984.

3.   <u>Television Wales - The New Industry, 1982-1987</u>: Cardiff, S4C, 1988.

The Welsh in Australia:
a bibliography

Ceris Gruffudd

Introduction

This bibliography, started in 1982 following a visit to Australia when I visited libraries, museums and archives to review material of Welsh interest, has been expanded as a result of dealing with readers' enquiries at the National Library of Wales and also by the addition of items published for and since the Australian Bicentennial (1988).

The bibliography deals specificially with Australia, although there are passing references to New Zealand. Books, periodical articles and theses are included together with manuscripts specific to the subject divisions. No attempt has been made however, to include all manuscripts as these are listed in Phyllis Mander Jones' Manuscripts in the British Isles relating to Australia, New Zealand and the Pacific. (Canberra, 1972) and in the Australian Joint Copying Project's Handbook.

The entries have been listed alphabetically under seven subject headings - Transportation, Diary and Letters, Genealogy, Travel and

Description, Religion, 'The Welsh in Australia', and Biographical. The entries for books comprise the author's name, book title, place of publication, publisher's name, year of publication and pagination. Entries for journal articles contain author's name, title of article, name of journal, volume and part number, and date of publication.

The biographical entries at the end list Australian Welsh people in volumes 1-11 of the <u>Australian Dictionary of Biography</u> (ADB) and the <u>Dictionary of Welsh Biography up to 1940</u>. Names in square brackets indicate second generation Welsh Australians or persons born outside Wales.   The Welsh in Australia did not have, unlike their counterparts in the United States of America, a flourishing publishing industry and the early period produced only two periodicals - <u>Yr Australydd</u> (1866-72) and <u>Yr Ymwelydd</u> (1874-76), both published in Victoria. Bob Owen, antiquary and book-collector, lists <u>Yr Ymgeisydd</u> as having been published in Castlemaine in 1865, but no copies have survived.

The only book of Welsh interest that I came across having been published in Australia during the last century is John Jones Thomas (Caraddaeg)'s <u>Britannia antiquissima: or a key to the philology of history (sacred and profane)</u>; Melbourne: Henry Tolman Dwight, 1860. 2nd edition, 1866.

A note in the NSW State Library reads, "The author seeks to prove from a study of the Welsh language and Welsh traditions that the Welsh of Cymry are indentical with the Cimmerians and that these were prehistoric civilized people in Europe and Asia Minor". The note "end of the first vol" on p. 216 is the only indication that there was to be another volume. Only the first volumes of both editions are listed in the British Library, National Libraries of Australia and Wales, the Mitchell Library, Sydney, and in Ferguson's Bibliography of Australia.

John Jones Thomas was born in Llanbadarn Fawr, Aberystwyth and according to Yr Ymwelydd I (1874/5), p. 191, was the brother of Mesac Thomas (later Bishop of Goulburn, NSW); John Jones Thomas is described on the title page as 'late Her Majesty's Inspector of Denominational Schools'.

There are three manuscript collections in the National Library of Australia (NLA) containing material on the Welsh in Australia. The Evan Thomas Collection, N301.453429 E92 comprises seven boxes and four volumes of material assembled by Evan Thomas. Thomas, born in Ysbyty Ifan, was for many years the secretary of the Cambrian Society of Victoria. The records of the Society and associated societies were preserved by him and are also in the NLA; MSS. 2595.

Mrs Olwen Watson, of Sydney, donated her parents' papers to the National Library of Australia in 1983 - the Maldwyn Rees Papers;

MS6781.   Blodwen and Maldwyn Rees had been active in Welsh life in Australia and were responsible for editing and publishing The Welsh Australian (1935-42).

I would welcome receiving any information regarding additions to the bibliography.

Ceris Gruffudd,
National Library of Wales, Aberystwyth, Dyfed, SY23 3BU, Wales.
January 1991.

Transportation

BEDDOE, Deirdre. Eleanor James: Cardiganshire's only female transportee to Australia. Ceredigion 8^3 (1978) 320-22

BEDDOE, Deirdre.   Carmarthenshire women and criminal transportation to Australia, 1787-1852. Carmarthenshire Antiquary 13 (1977) 65-71

BEDDOE, Deirdre. Carmarthenshire's convict women in nineteenth century Van Diemen's Land. Carmarthenshire Antiquary 15 (1979) 67-74

BEDDOE, Deirdre. Welsh convict women: a study of women transported from Wales to Australia, 1787-1852.   Barry: Stewart Williams, (1979) 166p.
Appendix lists transportees by county p.155-63
Short bibliography, p.165-6

FROST, John. The horrors of convict life. London (1856) 24p.
Two lectures delivered in the Oddfellows Hall, Padiham, August 31, 1865.
Another ed Hobart: Sullivan's Cove, 1973 65p Lim. ed. of 150 copies.

GILLEN, Mollie. The founders of Australia: a biographical dictionary of the First Fleet. Sydney: Library of Australian History, 1989 608p
'Welsh First Fleeters' listed on p. 423

HINDE, Joyce. From Amlwch via Chester to Australia. Gwreiddiau Gwynedd Roots 15 (Nov 1988) 20-21

JONES, E. Vaughan. Sheep stealing at Llangelynin 1792. Journal of the Merioneth Historical and Record Society VII^4 (1976) 384-403

JONES, Mair. Tocyn un ffordd. Pais Tachwedd 1988 18-19

JONES, Mair. Transported beyond the sea... Country Quest January
    1988 26, 29
Frances Williams, born Whitford, was on the First Fleet.

JONES, Peter M. S. More about a "Becca" character Carmarthenshire
    Historian XX (1985) 48-57
David Jones, one of the rioters who attacked Pontarddulais toll house
was transported to Van Diemen's Land.

MORRIS, E. Ronald. Montgomeryshire Chartist prisoners transported
    to Australia 1839. Powys Family History Society Cronicl 19
    (Autumn 1988) 51-58

OWEN, Brian.   Ishmael Jones - a Montgomeryshire murderer. Powys
    Family History Society Cronicl 23 (Winter 1990) 40-50

OWEN, Hugh J. From Merioneth to Botany Bay. Bala: R. Evans and
    Son, 1952 viii, 100p

PEARMAN, Anne.   The Third Fleet Convicts: a review and digest.
    Hel Achau 31 [Summer 1990] 11-13
Local (i.e. Clwyd) convicts on the Third Fleet.

PHILLIPS, Gwylon. Llofruddiaeth Shadrach Lewis. Llandysul: Gwasg
    Gomer, 1986 xviii, 183p
Bibliography p. 178-83

PHILLIPS, Gwylon. Y daith i Oz. Y Faner, 5.2.1988 18-19

RADFORD, Frances. The King against Elizabeth Jones and Catherine
    Jones. Gwreiddiau Gwynedd Roots 15 (Nov 1988) 11-12

SOUTTER, Sylvia. How two families moved to Australia because of 8s
    6d or 42¹/₂ new pence. Glamorgan Family History Society
    Journal 17 ([December] 1988) 23-5

TWISTON-DAVIES, Suzanne. Unwillingly from Monmouthshire to
    New South Wales. Presenting Monmouthshire 24 (1967) 30-31
Monmouthshire transportees in 1833.

WILLIAMS, David. <u>John Frost: a study in Chartism.</u> Cardiff:
University of Wales Press Board, 1939 viii, 355p

Letters/Diaries etc.

DAVIES, Owen. In search of gold: [letter from Owen Davies of Edern (from Spring Creek, Ovens Diggings) to John & David Davies of Liverpool, 23.9.1853] Yr Enfys, 50 (Jan/Feb 1961) 17, 27

EAMES, Aled. Y fordaith bell. Caernarfon: Gwasg Gwynedd, [i'w gyhoeddi/ to be published, 1991] ca. 176p

EVANS, Robert. Account of a voyage to Australia in 1883. NLW Facs 431
Photocopy of typescript
Robert Evans (1857-1945) came from Rhyl, Co. Flint

EVANS, William. A letter to Australia 1888. Glamorgan Family History Society Journal 16 ([August] 1988) 19-20

EVANS, William Meirion. Tair wythnos yn Liverpool a Chymru. Cylchgrawn Hanes y Methodistiaid Calfinaidd 7 (1983) 43-52
From his 1865 diary while on a visit to Wales

FROST, John. Letter to his wife from Port Arthur in Van Diemen's Land, his place of settlement. Manchester: A Heywood, 1840 4p

HUMFFRAY, John Basson. Diary of J.B. Humffray on board the 'Star of the East' during a voyage to Australia, 1853; and other notes [7 July-15 Sept 1853] 146p
Original MS in Ballarat Library, Ballarat, Victoria, MS 921 Hum.
Xerox copy in La Trobe Library, State Library of Victoria, MS 7822

JENKINS, Joseph. Diary of a Welsh swagman 1869-1894; abridged and noted by William Evans. South Melbourne: Macmillan, 1975 xviii, 216p map

JENKINS, Mary. Letters from Mary Jenkins of Pentwyn, Craigberthlwyd, Quakers' Yard, Llanfabon Parish, Glamorgan, to her son, Meshach, living in NSW, Australia with his wife Catherine. Glamorgan Family History Society Journal 4

([August] 1984) 19-21, 5 ([December] 1984) 25-26, 6 ([April]
1985) 9-11, 8 ([December] 1985) 16

JONES, Owen.   Hen lythyron: Owen Jones, Forest Creek, Victoria,
Awstralia, 12 Mai 1858 at Ebenezer Thomas 1802-63, Eben
Fardd. Barn 162/3 (1976) 231-3

ROBERTS, Elizabeth Grace (ed). Anglesey family letters 1840-1935.
Liverpool: H.E.G. Roberts, 1976 126, 14, XIIp, geneal. tables

THOMAS, Mary.   The diary and letters of Mary Thomas (1836-1866)
being a record of the early days of South Australia; ed. by
Evan Kyffin Thomas. 2nd ed. Adelaide: W.K Thomas & Co,
1915 ii, 162p

THOMAS, Mesac. Letters from Goulburn: a selection of letters from
Mesac Thomas, first Bishop of Goulburn; ed. by B. Thorn.
Canberra: Diocese of Canberra and Goulburn, 1964 84p

THOMAS, William. Hen lythyr. Taliesin 36 (Gorffennaf 1978) 73-80

TWAIN, Mark.   A letter from Mark Twain. Brisbane: Shapcott Press,
1964 [7]p
Letter to Father David Morgan Jones, native of Wales. Original letter
in the University of Queensland Library

WARBUTON, David.   Diary of a Welsh emigrant.   Country Quest
August 1989 18-19
Selections from the log of David Warburton, from Newtown, Powys,
who emigrated in 1848

Genealogy/Family histories

BAYLIS, M.J. The Makeigs of Cardigan: Parkypratt and Sydney, New South Wales. Ceredigion 9² (1981) 174-80

BENTLEY, Mollie. Thomas Edwards of Beverley: immigrant, policeman, settler. Carlisle, WA: Hesperian Press, 1985 xiv, 101, [17]p., porst
Born in Welshpool, Montgomeryshire; to WA in 1857

BLACK, Ian. Migration to Australia. Glamorgan Family History Society Journal, 15 ([March 1988]), 27-28
David Jenkins' family from Coity emigrated to Melbourne in 1883

CHAPMAN, H.S. Welsh immigration to Australia: a case study Gwreiddiau Gwynedd Roots 8 (Spring 1985) 2-9, geneal. table

CROWLEY, Francis. British immigration to Australia, 1860-1914. Unpublished Ph.D. thesis, Oxford University, 1951.

DANIEL, Eva Doris. Grandfather was a Maldon pioneer. East Kew, Vic: E D Daniel, 1983 56p geneal. tables
Isaac Daniel's family emigrated from Monmouthshire

GREEN, Harry. Some Neath emigrants in the nineteenth century. Neath Antiquarian Society Transactions 1978 95-106, 1979 134-145 ports

GRIFFITHS, Martin J. Down under. Glamorgan Family History Society Journal 16, ([August] 1988) 23-24
Mainwaring family, Cwmavon, emigrated to NSW, 1860

HARRIS, Vera. Every life a picture: the autobiography of Daisy Vera Harris, née Peters. [s.l.]: The Press Gang, 1986. 72p ports.
Peters family from Flint town, emigrated to NSW, moved later to WA

HEARLE, Janet. The Thomas's "The Leicester": a 19th century family
of Bridgend. Glamorgan Family History Society Journal 16
([August] 1988) 3-6, 17 ([December] 1988) 10-15

LEPHERD, Frances. A Surrey Hills childhood: 1870 (The Frances
Lepherd Manuscript) ed. and with an introduction by Kenneth
and Elaine Moon and Terry Kass. [Armidale]: University of
New England Publishing Unit, 1981. xvii, 43p
The author's mother, Ann Lepherd (née Jones) emigrated to Sydney
from Cardiganshire in the mid 1850s.

MOON, Kenneth and Elaine Moon. The Frances Purcell Manuscript: a
Welsh childhood in New South Wales, 1870. National Library
of Wales Journal 22 (Summer 1981) 92-102

MOORE, Olive. Farr from Wales; compiled and written by Olive
Moore.   Ringwood East, Vic: Farr Family Reunion
Committee, 1988 vi, 59p.; geneal. tables, ports.
The family of Thomas Farr Jones of Llanfyllin, Montgomeryshire
emigrated in 1854

NEWMAN, Jennifer. Emigration from 19th century Wales with
particular reference to South Australia. Unpublished Honours
Degree Thesis in History, Flinders University of South
Australia, 1981.

PERROTTET, Anthony.   Drowning in the Murrumbidgee River
scheme. Geo 12^2 (June-Aug 1990) 52-59
An account of the Welsh who emigrated to Leeton, NSW from
Patagonia, Argentina in the early 1900s

PHILIPPS, A. No borrowed gold. Perth, WA: Access Press, 1982 161p
Autobiography of a Welsh migrant who settled in Western Australia in
1920s: set mainly in Kojonup area

PIONEERS of the North West Plains, volume II; compiled by Kath
Mahaffey. Moree: Moree and District Historical Society, 1982
121p
Jones family from Co Radnor, Wales, p. 74-6
Williams family from Brynaman. Glamorganshire, p. 114-117

SCALE, Grant.   The Scale family of Pembrokeshire and Australia.
Alexandria, Vic.: G.Scale, 1990.   175p, geneal. tables, maps,
ports
Bibliography p.174-5

TEMPLE, Margaret. Goers & Shicers: early days at Moonlight.
Castlemaine: Castlemaine Mail [1980?] [76]p
Lewis family, originally from Bala, emigrated to Victoria in 1854

THOMAS, Norman.   From Bendigo and Tarnagulla to Dolau Cothi.
Neath Antiquarian Society Transactions 1988/9 p.99-101

WILLIAMS, Lesley, Dorothy Moffat & Thomas Ll. Williams.   If the
Leichhardt tree could talk; an account of the establishment of
the Williams family in Mackay, Queensland, by Lesley
Williams, with contributions by Dorothy Moffat (née
Williams), Thomas Ll. Williams of Bangor, North Wales and
other members of the family. Tamborine North, Queensland:
L.M. Williams, 1987 328p geneal. tables, ports
The descendants of John Henry Williams of Bethesda and Bangor

ZRNA, Bronwyn. Some Welshmen in Victoria, Australia in 1888. Hel
Achau, 15 (Spring 1985) 19-23

Travel books and Descriptions

D ap G ap Huw Feddyg
See PUGHE, David William.

DAVIES, Gareth Alban. Dyddiadur Awstralia.   Abertawe: Ty John
Penry 1986 133p

DAVIES, Jonathan Ceredig. Awstralia Orllewinol. Treorchy: Tom J.
Davies, 1903 120p

DAVIES, Jonathan Ceredig. Life, travels and reminiscences of
Jonathan Ceredig Davies. Llanddewi-brefi: the author, 1927
XVI,438p

DAVIES, Jonathan Ceredig. Western Australia: its history and
progress. Nantymoel: T. Evans, printer, 1902 119p

DAVIES, Mair Eluned. Ymweld ag Awstralia. Y Cylchgrawn
Efengylaidd, 18 (1980) 200-5

GRIFFITH, John Jones. Llythyrau hen forwr: sef llythyrau Capten J.J.
Griffith at ei wyr; dan olygiaeth y Parch R.W. Davies.
Lerpwl: Hugh Evans a'i Feibion, 1933 t. 33-38

HUGHES, Josiah. Australia revisited in 1890. London: Simpkin,
Marshall, Hamilton, Kent and Co; Bangor: Nixon and Jarvis,
1891 xvi, 499p

HUMFFRAY, John Basson. Ballaratania 1881-3; an answer to a
Londoner's question: "What sort of a place is this Ballarat?"
Ballarat: Campbell Pr., 1883 14p

JONES, Goronwy Rhys. 'Adenydd colomen pe cawn ...' Cennad 4[2]
(Hydref 1983) 21-8
The author's experiences while working as a doctor amongst the
Aborigines, 1980-1

JONES, William. Teithiau Wil Tyddyn. [Porthmadog]: Ty ar y Graig, 1977 169p

PUGHE, David William 'D ap G ap Huw Feddyg' . Gwlad yr aur; neu, gydymaith yr ymfudwr Cymreig i Australia. Caernarfon: H. Humphreys, [1852?] 52p

QUEENSLAND. London: Swyddfa Ymfudiaeth y Llywodraeth i Queensland, [1866?] 52p

RICHARDS, Alun. The wizardry of Oz. Quadrant XXXIII[252] (Jan-Feb 1989) 95-7

STEPHENS, J. Oliver. Blwyddyn yn Awstralia. Dysgedydd, 110 (1931) 51-4, 71-5, 107-12, 186-90, 364-6; 111 (1932) 16-20, 71-7

THOMAS, R. D. 'Iorthyn Gwynedd'. Yr ymfudwr, yn cynnwys hanes America ac Australia, yn nghyda phob hyfforddiant i ymfudwyr arg gan H Parry, Drefnewydd, 1854 117p
'Australia' p. 98-106

TREFEDIGAETH Australia: crynodeb o ammodau y llywodraeth i ... sefydlwyr ... ar Afon yr Alarch. Cardigan: J Davies, 1829

WILLIAMS, Hugh. Robinson Crusoe Cymreig, sef hanes mordaith i Awstralia. Caernarfon: John Williams [1857] iv, 3-103p

WILLIAMS, John, 'Glanmor'. Awstralia a'r cloddfeydd aur. Denbigh: T Gee, 1852 viii, 160p

WILLIAMS, W. Sylvanus. Atgofion o wlad bell. Haul Cyfres Dolgellau 33 (1931) 294-7, 349-52; 34 (1932) 54-6

Religion

ACHOSION crefyddol Cymreig yn Awstralia. Y Beirniad XIV (1873)
146-58, 263-76, 338-47

1871-1971: one hundred years of fellowship: the history of the first
century of the Melbourne Welsh Church. Melbourne:
Melbourne Welsh Church, 1971 20p

EVANS, William Meirion. Trem ar agwedd crefydd yn mysg Cymry
Victoria Awstralia. Cyfaill o'r Hen Wlad 27^{321} (Medi 1864)
276-8

G.E.P. Establishing Welsh Church in Sydney. Yr Enfys 41 (Oct/Nov
1958) 22

JENKINS, William Rhys. Carmel Welsh Presbyterian (CM) Church,
Sebastopol: centenary: 1861-1961; 100 years of witness.
Ballarat, Vic: Carmel Welsh Presbyterian Church, [1961] [8]p.

JONES, Emyr Gwynne. Annibynwyr Cymraeg Awstralia. Y Cofiadur
26 (1956) 3-40 map

JONES, Emyr Gwynne. The Welsh Independents (Congregationalists)
of Australia. Church Heritage 3^3 (March 1984) 238-276
An English translation of 'Annibynwyr Cymraeg Awstralia'.

LEWIS, L.D. 1883-1933 Jubilee celebrations: history of the United
Welsh Church of Blackstone, Queensland, Australia.
Blackstone: United Welsh Church of Blackstone, 1933 19p

MALDON Congregational Church 1858-1977. Maldon: Maldon
Congregational Church, 1977 [11]p

OWEN, Bob. Bedyddwyr Cymreig Awstralia, 1851-80. Trafodion
Cymdeithas Hanes Bedyddwyr Cymru 1960 42-50

REES, Horatio. A short history of the Welsh Presbyterian Church, Chalmers Street, Sydney. Y Wawr=The Dawn: newsletter of the Welsh Church Melbourne March 1988 p. 1-4

SAVILL, B.J. The Welsh Church - Latrobe Street, Melbourne: a brief history. Melbourne: Royal Historical Society of Victoria, [1988?]10p; typescript. C M Archives PX 2/1/9

STEPHENS, J. Oliver. Yr Eglwys Wesleaidd yn Awstralia. Yr Eurgrawn 123 (Medi-Hydref 1931) 335-41, 379-85

STEPHENS, J. Oliver. Henaduriaid Cymreig Awstralia. Y Drysorfa 109 (Rhagfyr 1939) 447-52

WILLIAMS, Robert. A short history of the Welsh Calvinistic Church, Williamstown [ca 1865-96] 5 leaves.
Copy of unpublished manuscript account, NLW Facs 603.

General - "The Welsh in Australia"

Yr AWSTRALYDD Cymraeg = The Welsh Australian. [Canberra]:
Welsh Cambrian Society of the A.C.T., 1989 [16]p

BALLARAT EISTEDDFOD. Report of the meetings held in Ballarat in
1885-6, with introductory and historical notes; together with
the programme of the Eisteddfod to be held in 1887; ed. by
Theos. Williams and J.B. Humffray. Ballarat: James Curtis,
1886 27p

BENJAMIN, M. Gwyn. A history of the Cambrian (Welsh) Society of
South Australia, Incorportated, 1927-1982.   Adelaide: the
Society, 1982 [15] leaves; typescript.

BLACKSTONE-IPSWICH Cambrian Choir: a centenary history 1886-
1986. Blackstone: the Choir, [1988?] 32p

A CENTURY of eisteddfod tradition in Queensland. In Bi-Steddfod 88
Souvenir programme. Mackay, 1988 8-10

EAMES, Aled. The Australia connection = Awstralia, y cyfandir pell.
Gwynedd Archives & Museums Service, 1988 tête- bêche 23,
13

FAULL, Jim. South Australia's early mining heritage: the ethnic
contribution, Heritage Australia 3^2 (summer 1984) 70-73

HALDANE-STEVENSON, Patrick.   The Welsh in Australia.
Transactions of the Honourable Society of Cymmrodorion
1988 177-83

HUGHES, A. Festin. Welsh. In The Australian people: an
encyclopaedia of the nation, its people and their origins.
Sydney: Angus & Robertson, 1988 840-5

JENKINS, Evan D. & Arthur J. Jenkins. The golden chain: a history of Sebastopol with special reference to gold and mining. Sebastopol: Arthur J. Jenkins, 1980 [8], 136

JONES, E. Vernon. Australia's Llandeilo flag. Carmarthenshire Historian XVII (1980) 84 ill.

JONES, E. Vernon. More about the other Llandilo. Carmarthenshire Historian XVI (1979) 69-70

LLOYD, Lewis. Australians from Wales. Gwynedd Archives, 1988 282p map

LLOYD, Lewis. Destination Australia. Cymru a'r Môr=Maritime Wales 5 (1980) 146-50

LLOYD, Lewis. Merioneth and Australia - some historical connections. Journal of the Merioneth Historical and Record Society X^{iv} (1989) 306-24

LLOYD, Lewis. Passages to Australia: Welsh emigrants, master mariners and vessels. Cymru a'r Môr=Maritime Wales 7 (1983) 22-45

LLOYD, Lewis. A report on my recent researches in Australia. Cymru a'r Môr=Maritime Wales 12 (1989) 7-26

LUCAS, David. The Welsh, Irish, Scots and English in Australia. Australian Institute of Multicultural Affairs, 1987, 109 maps Bibliography p 76-92

MARTIN, Gillian & Ged Martin. Waltzing Britannia: a guide to Britain for Australians. Hale & Iremonger, 1989 Wales p 206-15

ROBERTS, G. Côr plant Cymry Awstralia [Charters Towers, Queensland] Cymru'r Plant X (1901) 195-6, 252 port

ROBINSON, F. & H.L. Skellern. Queensland eisteddfau (sic) In Queensland Eisteddfod Souvenir Programme. Brisbane, 1939 101-13

A WELSH copper-smelting works in Australia. South West Wales Industrial Archaeology Society Bulletin 51 (May 1990) 7-8

WILLIAMS, Myfi. Cymry Awstralia. Llandybïe: Christopher Davies, 1983 178p

Biographical

Llewelyn David Bevan
The LIFE and reminiscences of Llewelyn David Bevan, LL. B., DD.,
compiled and edited by Louisa Jane Bevan. Melbourne:
Wyatt and Watt, 1920 317 p., ports

PARKIN CONGREGATIONAL COLLEGE, Kent Town A book of
memory ... jubilee of Dr. Bevan's ministry, July 1865- July
1915 Adelaide: The College, 1915 24p

Jenkin Collier
PASSING of a plush-and-gas relic. Australasian Magazine 7 Sep 1954
28-30
Werndew, a 30 room Victorian style mansion in the fashionable
Melbourne suburb of Toorak, about to be demolished was built by
Welshman Jenkin Collier. The National Art Gallery of Victoria
acquired some of the furniture and architectural features (such as the
window settings and tiled fireplaces depicting a number of Welsh
country scenes) as museum examples of Victorian domestic styles.

Sir Owen Cox.
FULL freights for every ship...Sir Owen Cox plans ideal sea trade.
Transport by land and sea August 1918 16-17 port

SIR Owen Cox. Australasian Business Mar 1921 12-13

Sir Edgeworth David
DAVID, M.E. Professor David; the life of Sir Edgeworth David
London: Edward Arnold, 1937 320p

David Davies
DAVIES, David. 'My story, my work and people I have met'. An
autobiography 1879-1960. 1 microform reel, negative
(MICROFILM FM 412661) Mitchell Library, Sydney.
Written between 1948 and 1960, the autobiography refers to Davies'
early life in Wales (born, Pontarddulais), his arrival in Kalgoorlie in
1911 where he ws a miner. He later acted as Congregational Minister
in Western Australia and New South Wales.

David John Davies
LOANE, Marcus L. A centenary history of Moore Theological College.
    Sydney: Angus & Robertson, 1955 ix, 228p
Chapter 9: David John Davies, 1911-1935 p. 113-138

TWENTY-ONE years' principalship of Moore College, Archdeacon D.
    J. Davies. Sydney Diocesan Magazine Oct 1932 6-7

Sorobabel Davies
RICHARDS, Thomas. Sorobabel Davies (1806-77) Trafodion
    Cymdeithas Hanes Bedyddwyr Cymru 1955 57-60

WILLIAMS, Daniel Emrys. Sorobabel Davies Trafodion Cymdeithas
    Hanes Bedyddwyr Cymru 1975 30-36

J. Brenny Evans
Y PARCHG. J. Brenny Evans, Roma, Queensland Y Diwygiwr 53
    (1888) 230-34

William Meirion Evans
An English translation in manuscript of a biography of the Rev.
William Meirion Evans (1826-83), Calvinistic Methodist minister and
editor of Yr Ymwelydd and Yr Australydd.
Photocopy in NLW Facs 680; the original Welsh version has so far not
been located.

John Oliver Feetham
HAYHOE, A. John Oliver Feetham: a study of his life and influence in
    North Queensland 1913-1947. Unpublished Honours History
    Thesis, University of Queensland, 1968.

Sir Samuel Walker Griffith
GRAHAM, A. Douglas. The life of the Right Honorable Sir Samuel
    Walker Griffith, G.C.M.G., P.C. Brisbane: The Law Book Co
    of Australasia, 1939 105p (University of Queensland. John
    Murtagh Macrossan Lecture for 1938).

JOYCE, Roger B. Samuel Walker Griffith. St Lucia: University of
     Queensland Press, 1984 xi, 456p: ports
Bibliography p 412-25

VOCKLER, John C. Sir Samuel Walker Griffith.   Unpublished
     Honours degree in History Thesis, University of Queensland,
     1953

Owen Harries
EDWARDS, John. How Owen Harries leaned from left to right. The
     Bulletin 106 5436 (2 October 1984) 32-36

Jenkin Henry
HEARLE, Janet.   A Porthcawl benefactor. Glamorgan Family History
     Society Journal 21 ([April] 1990) 24-6

Frank Hughes
AUSTEN, Tom. The entombed miner. Perth, Western Australia: St
     George Books, 1986 214p
Bibliography p198-203
Divers, led by Welshman Frank Hughes, rescue a miner in Western
     Australia

J.B. Humffray
WILLIAMS, Theophilus.   An Australian Welshman. Wales 3 (1896)
     461-2

Joseph Jenkins
JONES, T. Llew. O Dregaron i Bungaroo. Llandysul: Gwasg Gomer,
     1981 114p
Copies published but later withdrawn on publisher's instructions

KNIGHT, Stephen.   The swagman from Trecefel. Planet 61 (1987)
     72-6

TRAMP o Gymro yn Awstralia. Bro 9 (1979) p [14-20]

Richard Lewis Jenkins
RICHARD Lewis Jenkins
In BARTLEY, Nehemiah. Australian pioneers and reminiscences 1849-
    1894. Sydney: John Ferguson, 1978 p. 144-8
Facsimile reprint: originally published Brisbane: Gordon & Gotch,
    1896

Joseph Bolitho Johns
ELLIOT, Ian. Moondyne Joe, the man and the myth. Nedlands:
    University of Western Australia Press, 1978 xiii, 172p
Bibliography p. 161-3

The LIFE, trial and execution of Joseph Johns, an associate of the
    notorious Captain Moonlight, who was sentenced to death at
    17 years of age, and reprieved; and nine years after was
    hanged, July 1885 for the attempted murder of a fellow
    prisoner. Hobart: William Higgins, 1885 4p

David Jones
IN Australia it's David Jones. Sydney: [David Jones?], 1952 16p

William Jones
RICHARDS, Thomas.   William Jones, Ballarat.   Y Llenor 21 (1942)
    86-90
Also reprinted in his Rhwng y silffoedd (1978) 105-9

Bill Lloyd
WILLIAMS, Katie. The Welshman who made it down under. Country
    Quest Jan 1990 22-3

Alfred Edward Morgans
Mr Alfred Edward Morgans
In REID, G. S. & M.R. Oliver. The Premiers of Western Australia;
    1890-1982. University of Western Australia Press, 1982 24-6

Dafydd Morris
TUDUR AP HYWEL. Bywgraphiad o'r diweddar Dafydd Morris,
    Ballarat. W.B. Macdonald. [s.d.]

Pixie O'Harris
O'HARRIS, Pixie. Our small safe world: recollections of a Welsh childhood. Sydney: Boobook Publications, 1986 xiv, 215, xv-xxii p
Bibliography p.xv-xvii

O'HARRIS, Pixie. Was it yesterday? Rigby: Adelaide, 1983 119p
Bibliography p. 117-9

John Oliver
NORMAN, James. John Oliver. North Queensland. Melbourne: General Board of Religious Education for the Church of England in Australia for the Diocese of North Queensland, [1953]

Tom Price
EDWARDS, Eric. Yr Anrhydeddus Tom Price. Yr Eurgrawn 169 (Gaeaf 1977) 154-9

GANZIS, Nicholas. Tom Price, First Labour Premier: a political biography. Unpublished Honours History Thesis, University of Adelaide, 1959

SMEATON, T.H. From stone cutter to Premier & Minister of Education: the story of Tom Price, a Welsh boy who became an Australian Statesman. Adelaide: Hunkin, Ellis & King, [1924] 244p

David Rees
CRAGO, Howard. David Rees - a father of Union. Hawthorn: Baptist Union of Victoria, 1985 [1], 12, [1] p

Thomas Richards
LLOYD, David Myrddin. An Australian literary pioneer from Dolgellau. Journal of the Welsh Bibliographical Society 6[6] (July 1949) 309-11

MILLER, Edmund Morris. Pressmen and governors Sydney: Sydney University Press, 1952 308p
Chapter III p. 93-117, 'Thomas Richards'

Robert Roberts
LAMB, Norman J. (ed) Robert Roberts, Y Sgolor Mawr. National
    Library of Wales Journal 4[3-4] (1945-46) 205-6
Two letters relating to Roberts' attempt to be licensed by the Bishop of
    Melbourne

David Samwell
BOWEN, E.G. David Samwell, 1751-1798 (Dafydd Ddu Feddyg).
    Cardiff: University of Wales Press, 1974 117p facsimile, map
Parallel Welsh text and English translation
Brief bibliography p. [117]

LEWIS, Wynne. Dafydd Ddu Feddyg. Cymru a'r Môr=Maritime Wales
    12 (1989) 29-33

George William Taylor
ELLIS, Gordon. The apprentice draper who became a millionaire.
    Country Quest Feb 1988 16-17

David John Thomas
DAVID John Thomas. Australian Medical Journal 16 (1871) 187-190

Lewis Thomas
PARRY, Nerida A. The Brynhyfryd story. Unpublished thesis, 1979
    NLW Facs 429.

Mesac Thomas
WYATT, Ransome T. The history of the diocese of Goulburn. Sydney:
    Edgar Bragg, 1937 385p
Chapter V, Mesac Thomas, first Bishop of Goulburn, 46-60
Bibliography p. 369-70

John Williams
WILLIAMS, John. So ends this day. Globe Press, 1981 [12] 226, [5]p

William Williams
ELLIS, Bryn. William Williams (1839-1915), arloeswr o Fôn.
    Transactions of the Anglesey Antiquarian Society 1971-72,
    111-29 geneal. table, English summary

Zephaniah Williams
BRIGGS, Asa. Chartists in Tasmania: a note. Bulletin of the Society for the Study of Labour History 3 (Autumn 1961) 4-8

WILLIAMS, David. Zephaniah Williams: a note. Bulletin of the Society for the Study of Labour History 5 (Autumn 1962) 43-44

A. C. Willis
YOUNG, I. E., A. C. Willis, Welsh nonconformist and the Labour Party in NSW 1911-33. The Journal of Religious History 2 1-4 (1962-3) 303-13

Howell Witt
WITT, Howell. Bush Bishop. Adelaide: Rigby, 1979 (vi), (7)- 237p

Welsh Australians in the Australian Dictionary of Biography vols. 1-11

Vol. No.

BAYLY, Nicholas	1
BEVAN, Llewelyn David	7
BIRKS, Frederick	7
BRACY, Henry	7
BRIGSTOCKE, Charles Ferdinand	1
BROWN, James	3
BRUNTNELL, Albert	7
BURGOYNE, Thomas	7
COLLIER, Jenkin	3
COX, Sir Edward John Owen	8
DAVID, Charles St. John	8
DAVID, Sir Tannat William Edgeworth	8
DAVIES, David, 1864-1939	8
DAVIES, David Mortimer	4
DAVIES William, 1882?-1956	8
DAVIS, Charles Henry	1
DOUGLAS, William Bloomfield	4
DUMARESQ, Edward	1
EVANS, George Essex	8
FEETHAM, John Oliver	8
FROST, John	1
GOODISSON, Lillie Elizabeth	9
GORDON, Margaret Jane	9
GOULD, Ellen Julia	9
GRANVILLE, Cecil Horace Plantagenet	9
GRIFFITH, Sir Samuel Walker	9
[GRIFFITHS, Philip Lewis]	9
[HARRIS, William]	9
HUGHES, William Morris	9
HUMFFRAY, John Basson	4
[IDRIESS, Ion Llewelyn]	9
JAMES, David	9

Welsh people with Australian connections in the Dictionary of Welsh Biography up to 1940 and its supplement

BEVAN, Llewelyn David
DAVID, Sir Tannat William Edgeworth
DAVIES, David, 1812?-74 'Dai'r Cantwr'
DAVIES, Jonathan Ceredig
DAVIES, Sorobabel
EVANS, William Meirion
FROST, John
GRIFFITH, Sir Samuel Walker
JONES, John Fl. 1811-58 'Shoni Sguborfawr'
JONES, Margaret
JONES, Thomas, 1819-82
PRICE, Thomas
RICHARDS, Thomas
RICHARDS, Robert, 1834-85 'Y Sgolor Mawr'
THOMAS, Lewis
THOMAS, Mesac
THOMAS, Robert David 'Iorthyn Gwynedd'
TREHARNE, Bryceson
WILLIAMS, John, 1811-91 'Glanmor'
WILLIAMS, Zephaniah

Welsh Australian Periodicals

Yr Australydd: cylchgrawn misol.
Smythesdale, Vic, 1 (1866) - 4 (1870); new series v.1 (April 1871) - 2 (Sept 1872)

The Cambrian
[Melbourne], 1[1] (November 1938)

The Cambrian: official journal of the Cambrian Society of Victoria
Melbourne, 1 (1939/40) - 6 (1946)

Carmelight: [magazine of] Carmel [Sebastopol, Ballarat, Victoria]
Welsh Presbyterian Church
Sebastopol, 1980 -

Y Ddolen: the news link of the Welsh Presbyterian Church of Sydney
Sydney, 1 (August 1965) - 2 (Dec 1965)

Llais: cylchgrawn y Gymdeithas Gymreig, Sydney
Sydney, 1 (1969/70) - 15 (1983)

Y Llythyr Newyddion = News Letter: newsletter of the Australian
Association of Welsh Societies
Thornbury, Vic, 1 (1932-6)

Sglodion; ed by Gareth D Evans
Melbourne: Gareth D Evans, 1 (March 1962) - [10? April?]
1965

Y Wawr = The Dawn: newsletter of the Welsh Church, Melbourne
Melbourne, 1 (Chwefror/February 1964) -

The Welsh Australian
Sydney 1 (1935/39) - 2 (1939/42)

Yr Ymwelydd: newyddiadur Cymreig at wasanaeth y Cymry yn
Australia, New Zealand etc
Melbourne, 1 (1874/5) - 2 (1876)

WELSH STUDIES